FAMILY HARAMBEE!

How to Discuss Potentially Challenging Discoveries in Your Family Tree: A Workbook

Kathy Lynne Marshall

Book Cover by Kathy "Kanika" Marshall

Kanika Marshall Arts & Books Publishing
PO Box 1202
Elk Grove, CA, 95758
KathyLynneMarshall.com

Printed in the United States of America

ISBN: 9781737573326 paperback
ISBN: 9781737573333 eBook

Dedication

Dedicated to the generations of my Black and White ancestors

who survived the rigors of their time,

paving the way for present generations to live our best life.

Acknowledgements

Innumerable thanks go to seventeen of my relatives who took a DNA test and placed their trust in me to carefully handle their results and write well-researched history books about our family.

Without the selfless generosity of the African American genealogy community, especially, I would not have become successful at finding information about our formerly enslaved ancestors. While there are too many to name individually, I salute the instructors from the Midwest African-American Genealogical Institute, and everyone who maintains a social media page dedicated to our ancestors and DNA research.

Thanks to the stalwarts who disseminate genealogy information via genealogy conferences, organizations, podcasts and Zoom presentations. Without help from these sources, I would still be throwing disorganized documents into a box, instead of turning them into stories and books that could be read and enjoyed.

And thanks to my Arthur Platform Coach, Ms. Joey Garcia, who nudged me to write this workbook to help others communicate all types of genealogy findings with their families.

Books by Kathy Lynne Marshall

Finding Marshalls: A Genealogy Trip with a Black and White Twist

The Marshall Legacy in Black and White

The Mystery of Margaret Booker

Finding Daisy: From the Deep South to the Promised Land

Finding Otho: The Search for Our Enslaved Ancestors

The Ancestors Are Smiling!

Ken Anderson: Alias Special K

Available at KathyLynneMarshall.com

Dear Reader,

This workbook is a product of love, resulting from decades of family history research that stretches across the United States into Africa, Europe and Asia. My passion is helping others find their ancestors.

I have written several award-winning heritage books that teach others how to conduct thorough historical research, interview elders about their ancestors and family lore, use DNA testing to sleuth additional relatives, manage uncomfortable family secrets, and leave a written legacy of diversity and inclusion that enhances the American historical record.

Maybe you are a full-fledged genealogist who has already written your family history and handled potentially challenging discoveries in your family tree. However, maybe you know of other relatives or friends who have no clue how to get started. Suggest they buy my biographies which tell fact-based stories, written from the point of racial groups who have contributed to our American heritage. Help me help others get a sense of how they may leave a legacy for their children. My books can help. Contact me for more information.

Thank you,

Kathy Lynne Marshall
KathyLynneMarshall.com

Table of Contents

List of Forms

Form Name	Step	Page
Potluck Sign-in Sheet for the Family Harambee	2	18
Harambee Child Sign-In Sheet	2	20
Committee Fees Questionnaire	4	27
DNA Informed Consent Agreement	5	32
Which Family Members Took a DNA Test?	5	43
Sample Letter Transmitting Family Report Forms Before Harambee	7	50
Family Records Sheet 1 (Partner1/Spouse 1 and Partner2/Spouse 2)	7	51
Family Records Sheet 2 (Children)	7	52
Family Records Sheet 3 (Request for Family Stories)	7	53
Family Group Email Test Message	11	63
Schedule of Events Itinerary	13	66
Master of Ceremonies Opening Speech	14	75
Master of Ceremonies Concluding Speech	15	81
Sample Letter Inviting Family to the Harambee	15	83

Introduction

Harambee!

How to Discuss Potentially Challenging Discoveries
in Your Family Tree: A Workbook

Harambee means "all pull together" in Kiswahili,
Kenya's national language

Breaking bread with kin could lead to common ground, reconciling past wrongs and hurts, and forming new familial friendships—even when the topics of conversation are taboo. During her genealogical research, Kathy Marshall discovered White family members in Georgia, the descendants of the man who once owned Kathy's ancestors. Her cousin, the slave owner's 6th great-granddaughter, was aghast that her family had owned Black people; she wanted to atone for their actions by lending Kathy moral support and information from her family tree. The two women set out for the back roads of Georgia, exploring cemeteries, courthouses and former plantations, and meeting with other Black and White cousins along the way.

Through wide-ranging and vulnerable conversations, they came to grips honestly with America, its weaknesses and its strengths. Kathy felt so strongly about the different perspectives on race, gender, and lineage that she wrote a separate book about the genealogy trip, *Finding Marshalls: A Genealogy trip with a Black and White Twist*. What follows are potential steps you could consider for convening a family event to discuss your ancestral lineage. Getting together family members from disparate racial groups, religious backgrounds, political ideologies, or gender identification may cause a blossoming of understanding a variety of points of view.

On the flip side, some topics may be difficult, uncomfortable, or inappropriate for all ages. There might be strong opinions and arguments, especially if some relatives cling to old versions of the family story or cultural history.

Kathy handled most of the Family Harambee tasks alone during her travels to research her family's genealogy, including convening several small meetings pre-and post-trip. If you expect more than a dozen attendees, consider having several people help you make your event a success. The guidelines in this workbook may also be useful for convening a full family reunion, an intimate conversation among cousins at a restaurant, or an online family chat session.

Step 1: Assemble Core Committee to Discuss Action Steps

Organize a small committee to manage the Family Harambee. At their initial meeting, they can choose a project leader; discuss the steps necessary to convene a meeting of the minds among family members; fine-tune the list of duties presented in this book; identify a theme and purpose; and gather volunteers to implement necessary tasks outlined in Step 2. For events with fewer than 12 people, one person might handle most tasks, as Kathy did for gatherings based on her books, *The Marshall Legacy in Black and White* and *Finding Marshalls: A Genealogy Trip with a Black and White Twist*. For larger groups, one committee member could be assigned for every twenty participants.

Leader: The committee leader should be a person who has excellent communication skills, is empathetic, impartial, and trustworthy. The leader should be able to read people well and adjust their behavior and mannerisms in response to body language and tone of voice. The topics discussed in the committee and the Family Harambee will entail complicated and emotional issues that must be handled respectfully.

Genealogist: It is also crucial to have a genealogist or family historian on the committee. This should be someone who has studied the family lineage and compiled research in written form. This individual can prepare the committee to handle challenging topics that might arise. A genealogist is defined by Merriam-Webster as "a person who traces or studies the descent of persons or families." A family historian is a person who writes and compiles stories about their ancestor's lives.

One person could do all those tasks. Genealogist responsibilities include compiling family data forms (Step 7); building the family tree (Step 8); organizing the genealogy data into binders, booklets, or books to be made available to family members (Step 9). The genealogist could also supervise volunteers tasked with clerical functions. The genealogist would work hand-in-hand with the family DNA expert (or they might be the same person). The genealogist and the DNA expert should be available to answer questions during the Family Harambee meeting and any subsequent Zoom sessions.

Office: The third committee member could handle various clerical functions like capturing meeting minutes, emailing family members about upcoming events, and making phone calls. This person could work closely with the genealogist to help input family contact and historical data into a computer and assemble family history booklets for the Family Harambee. This person should be comfortable using computers, be detail-oriented, goal-oriented, reliable, and willing to complete tasks in a timely manner.

Other committee members could help the leader, genealogist and office members, and handle general tasks such as helping set up a reception table at the Harambee, assisting family members in a variety of ways, cleaning up, etc.

Committee members would decide on family memorabilia, such as T-shirts, hats, buttons, pens, etc., for the Harambee theme (include the year and place on items).

Committee members: Write the name, email, and phone number of core members. Remember, they should be committed people who will help implement the plans.

Leader:_____

_____

Genealogist:_____

_____

Office:_____

_____

Other:_____

_____

_____

_____

_____

Step 2. Gather Volunteers to Support the Committee

Several months before the Family Harambee, the committee should send out an email request seeking family volunteers to help plan and produce the Family Harambee. Select volunteers based on the committee's knowledge of their skills and ability to commit and follow through on tasks. You don't want family squabbles to erupt over someone's incomplete task, or for the Harambee to feel like a burden.

For small gatherings of 12 people or fewer, one family member knowledgeable about genealogy could easily manage most of the following functions solo.

DNA Expert: Analyze the DNA test results for whoever tests, and produce charts, graphs, and narratives that everyone could understand. A genealogist might do this job.

Write the name, email, and phone number of the DNA expert:

_____

_____

General Helpers: Help the genealogist input contact information and family data into an online or private computer database. These workers could also purchase name tags, maintaining meeting attendee contact information, printing the agenda and meeting minutes. They would email a summary of the in-person Family Harambee and any Zoom meetings that followed. They could also assist at the gathering, setting up the reception table and cleaning up afterwards.

Write the name, email and phone number of the general helpers:

_____

_____

_____

_____

Zoom Meeting Coordinator: Responsible for scheduling Zoom calls with family members before and after the Harambee. The coordinator must be comfortable handling technical issues with the Zoom call, including how to record and download the session so others can watch it later. The Zoom Coordinator must be patient and skilled at helping technophobes and those who are not Zoom-literate. People will need help to understand how to mute and unmute themselves, turn on their video so other participants can see them, and how to take part in the chat, if that is a part of the meeting. The Zoom Coordinator must also be familiar with both PCs and Macs to offer support for both platforms.

Write the name, email, and phone number of the Zoom coordinator:

_____

_____

Cultural Coordinator: Work with the genealogist to identify potential conflicts based on the family history data that has been uncovered. The coordinator must be compassionate, calm, thoughtful, and able to de-escalate tensions. They should be prepared to moderate conversations that broach distressing extremes in the subjects of race, politics, religion, sexual identity, among others. Someone with professional de-escalation skills would be helpful. They should also become familiar with the Coming to the Table organization (comingtothetable.org) to learn mitigating strategies for dealing with uncomfortable issues which might disrupt the Harambee. Coming to the Table's motto is: "working together to create a just and truthful society that acknowledges and seeks to heal from the racial wounds of the past, from slavery, and the many forms of racism it spawned." They deal exclusively with the emotional issues that might occur between racial and other groups.

The cultural coordinator should review the discussions in the Car Talk Chapter, Steps 12 and 13 of Kathy Marshall's *Finding Marshalls: A Genealogy Trip with a Black and White Twist* to gain an idea of the taboo conversations shared by Kathy and other racially diverse cousins during her trip to Georgia. These conversations often centered on personal or cultural wounds, such as:

- My ancestors owned people? What is my responsibility for that, if any?
- Why are so many Black women angry?
- What explains continued economic disparities between Blacks and Whites?
- Why do some feel slave owners are portrayed negatively?
- Why do some bristle at teaching the contribution of all groups of people who have made America a great nation?

The Cultural Coordinator should be prepared to make a presentation of their method and findings at the Harambee. This may include preparing a PowerPoint-type presentation so all participants can see the research and results. See more duties in Step 11.

Write the name, email, and phone number of the cultural coordinator:

_____

_____

Master of Ceremonies: Open the meeting, introduce the speakers, and make sure the program flows according to the agenda prepared by the Family Harambee committee. The master of ceremonies should be engaging, have a sense of humor yet be respectful, able to maintain control of the Harambee, able to place participants at ease, and smile aplenty.

Write the name, email, and phone number of the master of ceremonies:

_____

_____

Photographer or videographer: Record all aspects of the Harambee, including family stories from the elders or others, and clearly label the photos and videos. They should

15

have the necessary equipment, skill and ability to capture group and individual family shots, and they would make this material available to family members for a negotiated fee. Event photographs should be stored in an archive for future retrieval.

Write the name, email and phone number of the photographer or videographer:

_____

_____

Site Coordinator: Handle issues related to accommodations, such as interacting with hotel staff or family members who have agreed to provide lodging. The Site Coordinator should negotiate a "package deal" to get the best room rates, free breakfast, free parking. They should manage bedrooms and meeting rooms. This should be a calm person who can handle sometimes demanding, unhappy relatives while juggling several crises at a time. It would be helpful if this person had attended or arranged similar functions in the past. In that way, they would have a good idea of what to expect. Write the name, email and phone number of the site coordinator:

_____

_____

Storyteller(s): Tell interesting, fun, and emotional family stories. Controversial or titillating material could be kept to adults-only spaces later in the evening. Storytellers should be engaging and animated, not babbling, not rambling, nor using a monotonous voice. The committee should interview storyteller volunteers and have them recite one or two stories to determine whether they would be suitable for the Family Harambee.

Write the name, email, and phone number of the storyteller(s):

_____

_____

Food Coordinator and helpers: Negotiate a "package deal" with a restaurant to determine a variety of menu selections (e.g., meat and vegetarian options) and how payment would be rendered. This person would work with the Harambee's volunteer clerical staff to type up meal options to be sent or emailed to family members, including instructions on how to choose their meal selection and pay in advance.

The committee could contract with a caterer, ensuring that they taste the product in advance; negotiate prices; share the date, time, and itinerary; and maintain regular contact with the caterer. Care should be taken to ensure the menu has foods everyone can eat, including traditional "soul food" and healthier options.

For non-restaurant Harambee gatherings, the food coordinator could plan and execute the menu, with committee input. This may include coordinating potluck meals, beverages, eating utensils, plates, etc. And why not have a cooking competition?

Write the name, email and phone number of the food coordinator and helpers(s):

_____

_____

_____

_____

_____

If the Harambee is a potluck, a simple sign-in sheet might be all that's needed.

A slight modification of the potluck sign-up could assign the first letter of the family surnames to dictate which type of dish they should bring, for example:

A-F brings appetizers (e.g., Andersons and Bosks would bring appetizers).
G-L brings salad, vegetable or fruit dishes.
M-R brings a main dish like meat, casserole, or pasta dish.
S-Z brings a dessert.

Potluck Sign-in Sheet for the_____ **Family Harambee**

(Family name)

Sign your name and what food you will bring from the category below
(Your dish should feed at least #_____ people)

Name & Phone	Appetizer or Vegetable	Salad or Fruit	Main Dish	Dessert

Children's Activity Coordinator and helpers: Supervise young children while the adults circulate with each other. This person should be at ease with children, calm, friendly, able to lift a thirty-pound child. They should have a CPR and First Aid certification (check with your local community center for information on how to get these). There should be one coordinator for every six-to-ten school-aged children, with more direct supervision for infants and younger children.

Write the name, email and phone number of the child care coordinator and helpers(s):

_____

_____

_____

_____

_____

_____

Each child should be signed in on a Family Harambee Child Sign-in Sheet, including the child's name, their parent's name(s), parent's phone number, and any allergies or medical conditions the child may have.

The coordinator should plan to secure cribs or playpens for infants and toddlers, ask parents to leave diaper bags and appropriate bottles and formula, as needed. The coordinator should have a variety of child-appropriate games, soft balls, Nerf products, blankets, early reader books for storytelling, etc. The Centers for Disease Control suggests there be an emergency kit for various ages of children. For babies, that might include a well-stocked diaper bag (at least one pack of diapers, at least two packs of baby wipes, baby powder, diaper rash cream, baby wash and lotion, and re-sealable plastic bags (gallon size) for stashing dirty diapers and clothes. Also, ready-to-feed infant formula in single serving cans or bottles, burp rags or smaller blanket, hand sanitizers, pacifiers, teething gel, infant-safe pain reliever, bulb syringe, and snacks.

_____ Harambee Child Sign-In Sheet

Child Name	Parent(s)	Phone	Allergies or Medical issues
_____	_____	_____	_____
_____	_____	_____	_____
_____	_____	_____	_____
_____	_____	_____	_____
_____	_____	_____	_____
_____	_____	_____	_____
_____	_____	_____	_____
_____	_____	_____	_____
_____	_____	_____	_____
_____	_____	_____	_____
_____	_____	_____	_____
_____	_____	_____	_____
_____	_____	_____	_____
_____	_____	_____	_____
_____	_____	_____	_____
_____	_____	_____	_____
_____	_____	_____	_____
_____	_____	_____	_____
_____	_____	_____	_____
_____	_____	_____	_____
_____	_____	_____	_____
_____	_____	_____	_____
_____	_____	_____	_____
_____	_____	_____	_____

Get emergency contacts for where the Family Harambee is being held.

Fire emergency phone number: 911

Address: _____

_____

Closest Hospital or Urgent Care Clinic name, phone, and address:

_____

_____

_____

Restaurant name, phone, and address:

_____

_____

_____

Hotel name, phone, and address:

_____

_____

_____

Games Coordinator: Bring equipment for recreational activities for older children and adults like card games (UNO, spades), boardgames, basketball, corn hole, chess. If there is a swimming pool, ensure there's a volunteer to serve as a life guard.

Also, the games coordinator could create games and puzzles related to family history. Collect inexpensive prizes to give away to the winners of individual questions or to those who get the highest number of correct answers to the quiz.

Write the name, email and phone number of the history games coordinator:

_____

_____

Here are three examples of what the history games coordinator might create for different ages.

1. Purchase or create some historical black figure flash cards for younger children and give each child a card to read aloud, with the help of the coordinator. The cards could be safety-pinned to their chest or back so they can tell people which historical person they are representing. (Google "Historical black heroes for children" to view examples of the cards). *Black Heroes* is a good example.

2. Create a quiz for teenagers and adults based on your family history. Find questions by searching the family tree or findagrave.com or Google Family History Games. Here are some simple examples. The person with the highest number of correct answers might win an inexpensive prize or ribbon:

- Name all four of your grandparents.
- Name all eight of your great-grandparents.
- Where was your paternal grandfather born?
- How many siblings does your mother have?
- What is the name of the oldest living woman in your family?
- Who in your family had the most children?
- Where was your mother born?
- Which of your relatives lived to be the oldest?
- Who in your family went to college?
- Which relatives served in the military?
- Who are the family historians?

3. Create a quiz for teenagers and adults based on African American history (Google "African American history questions and answers"). Here are some simple examples. The person with the highest number of correct answers might win an inexpensive prize or ribbon:

- What color uniform did union soldiers wear during the Civil War?
- Which President signed the Emancipation Proclamation?
- When did the celebration of Black History Month begin? (the closest answer wins)
- Which woman took the most people from slavery to freedom?
- Who knows what year slavery was discontinued?
- What Constitutional Amendment gave Black men the right to vote?
- What year was Barack Obama voted President?
- Who is the first black woman to serve on the Supreme Court?
- When was the Civil Rights Act signed?
- Who was the first Black female astronaut?

Author: Work with the genealogist to incorporate the family history into a book and make it available for each family (maybe for a fee). Choose a format that works best for the information and your family's preferences, whether it be a paperback, photo book, three-hole-punch book in a binder, saddle-stitch stapled book, or e-book. The book may be distributed during the Harambee or afterward to ensure any sensitive issues have been ironed out before the book is printed. There's no need to publish the book on Amazon or any other site; this could be a private family legacy book.

Write the name, email and phone number of the author(s):

_____

_____

Social Media Coordinator: Document family events, collect photographs, and organize researched information for the family's private social media sites, like Meta-Facebook or Instagram. The social media coordinator should be comfortable using online sites and be willing to monitor and respond to messages. Social media posts might be about the genealogist's family research. Relatives and family historians could comment on posts, adding what they know about the ancestors, including stories, photographs, documents, DNA, or answer questions.

The social media coordinator could collaborate with the genealogist and author to produce a periodic blog. A blog is an online journal that could be another avenue for families to stay informed of exciting breakthroughs in ancestral research, or to collect family opinions, theories of parentage, or discuss other family mysteries.

Videos created during genealogy trips can be uploaded to a family YouTube site. Kathy uses Apple Computer's free iMovie app to turn smartphone video footage into movies that she uploads to YouTube. Genealogy research trips can be expensive, so providing virtual access to far-away events allows all family members to take part. Get ideas for your family videos by checking out Kathy's over 100 videos at (YouTube.com/user/Kanikaas).

Write the name, email, and phone number of the social media coordinator:

_____

_____

Step 3: Choose One Genealogical Line for the Harambee?

It might be helpful to focus the Harambee on one genealogical line at a time. This will make your experience more pleasant and manageable. For example, Kathy chose her grandfather, Austin Henry Marshall, as the individual to be highlighted in *The Marshall Legacy in Black and White*. Her goals were to find Austin's descendants, his parents and their slave-owning families. She also explored whether DNA testing could help her find additional blood relatives who might have factual information about her paternal Marshall family and the Smiths and Ligons who married into that line.

During Kathy's genealogy trip to Columbus, Georgia, (Austin's hometown), and to Talbot, Harris, and Putnam counties, she discovered where the Marshall slave owners had lived with her forced worker ancestors. She also followed clues uncovered at the Tuskegee Institute and courthouse that led to startling stories from the 1870s that mirrored present-day Georgia squabbles about voting and race. But it was the intimate, and sometimes difficult discussions on taboo topics with her Black and White blood relatives that fueled her book, *Finding Marshalls: A Genealogy Trip with a Black and White Twist* and this workbook.

- Decide which ancestor or family line should be discussed by the committee:

_____

_____

_____

_____

_____

_____

_____

Step 4. Determine Fees for the Harambee

Organizing a Family Harambee requires time and effort from many people. There may be out-of-pocket costs for printing family history booklets; deposits for reserving hotel rooms or restaurants; purchasing DNA tests; fee-based online resources to record family tree data; professional services to photograph or videotape the Harambee; and mailing invitations. There may be hundreds of hours expended to research the family lineage; input historical data into a database; analyze family and DNA information; prepare a meeting location; and record the Harambee.

You may decide to charter buses to transport family members from their homes to the Harambee, or to take participants around to side trips. You may secure a Travel Agent to assist family with their transportation needs.

One of the Committee's duties should be to decide whether families should be charged for some, all, or none of the expenses.

What follows is a sample survey that committee members could complete to help decide whether any fees should be charged to Harambee participants.

Committee to Determine Fees Questionnaire

Respondent Name: _____

Organizing a Family Harambee requires time and effort from many people. There may be out-of-pocket costs for printing family history booklets; deposits for reserving hotel rooms or restaurants; purchasing DNA tests; fee-based online resources to record family tree data; professional services to photograph or videotape the Harambee; and mailing invitations. There may be hundreds of hours spent to research the family lineage; input historical data into a database; analyze family and DNA information; prepare a meeting location; and record the Harambee. Do you want to charge families fees to cover these costs? Indicate your choices in the underlined spaces below.

_____ Yes or No: Committee members and volunteers should offer their services for free to better the entire Family Harambee. If No, how much should families be charged? $__

_____ Yes or No: The committee should pay a photographer or videographer to provide family group shots which may be used in a newsletter, on social media, and in a family book. (Take care to negotiate with the photographer regarding the number of photos or hours of video you desire). If Yes, decide in advance how much each Harambee participant would contribute toward the group photographs or any copies they may want. $_____

_____ Yes or No: Each family should pay for their own meal tab, **or,**

_____ Yes or No: The Committee should arrange for three different meals (e.g., red meat, poultry, and vegan meal). Each person would pay a set price for an adult or child's meal. Adult meals should be a maximum of $_____ and children $_____.

_____ Yes or No: Each family should be charged a maximum of $_____ to cover paper, printing, and mailing costs.

_____ Yes or No: Families would be charged $_____ for each Family Harambee T-shirt, $_____ for hats, $_____ for buttons created for the Harambee.

_____ Yes or No: Families should be charged for a 20-to-30-page family history booklet or pamphlet that is created for the Harambee?
If Yes, how much would be charged? $_____

_____ Yes or No: Families should be charged for paperback, hardback, or e-Book that is published after the Harambee and includes extensive genealogy research, stories, and family photographs? If Yes, how much would be charged? $_____

_____ Other fees? (list): _____

_____

_____

_____

_____

_____

_____

_____

_____

_____

_____

Step 5. Encourage Relatives to Take a DNA Test

A lot of emphasis will be placed on this topic because DNA results will help find blood relatives who may have useful, documented information about your family members. This undertaking must start many months before the Harambee, though, because it takes time to purchase, process the DNA, and analyze the results. Then the genealogist and committee will need to discuss how to handle any uncomfortable secrets that might arise before the Harambee.

Why is DNA Testing Useful?

When the paper trail of historical documents ran dry, Kathy turned to DNA testing to learn more about her lineage before, during, and after the period of slavery in America. She found additional blood relatives in her paternal Marshall line from DNA testing, which helped her find proof of all four paternal great-grandparents, their family's blood-related slave owners, and other descendants who took DNA tests. Once her family's former slave owners were determined, Kathy used traditional genealogical research to investigate their land, probate, and census records to determine where and how her formerly enslaved ancestors lived. DNA testing was integral to finding truths about Kathy's family and it might help you.

Your family challenges may not include slavery, but your issues may include adoptions, name changes over the generations which make it difficult to find historical information, interracial relationships, or official records that were burned in the local repositories where your family lived. DNA testing may be the magic that helps you piece together your lineage.

It is important to complete DNA testing as early as possible in the planning process. It can take six-to-eight weeks to receive the DNA results, then more time to analyze the results to try to find common ancestors with other people who tested. The great thing about DNA is that you will find lost relatives that will help fill out your tree and answer questions about your lineage. The bad thing about DNA is that you may discover lost relatives the family doesn't want to find (the next step will discuss what to do about troublesome truths found by DNA testing).

Here's a quick DNA primer to help explain why it's helpful to get your DNA family tested. Did you know that you get:

- 50% of your DNA from your mom and the other half from your dad?
- 25% from each of your four grandparents?
- 12.5% from each of your eight great-grandparents?
- 6.25% from each of your sixteen great-great-grandparents?

Encourage DNA Testers to Sign a DNA Consent Form

Police use DNA testing to catch crooks, murderers, and rapists who leave their genetic material at the scene of a crime. Some Baby Mamas use it to establish the paternity of their children. Rich people want to verify rights to inheritance. Some people want to learn about genetic medical conditions. But many people only take a DNA test to find out where in Africa or Europe or Asia their ancestors came from. They have no idea, nor do they care, that DNA testing can help us find blood relatives who can help us learn who our ancestors were. DNA doesn't lie, so as wonderful as it can be, DNA can reveal shocking surprises in the family tree.

Warning: Keep in mind there are many people searching for their family, such as: Adoptees or people who put their biological children up for adoption, Holocaust survivors who were unable to reconnect with any relatives after World War II, people from the Old Country whose names were changed when they came to America so they cannot easily locate ancestors, and people born using a sperm donation who are looking for information about their paternal (Y-DNA) side. Your DNA results may uncover some of these people in your family tree. It's important to let your family know the potential for finding unexpected family members through a DNA test.

Blaine Bettinger, author of the popular *The Genetic Genealogist* and *The Family Tree Guide to DNA Testing Genetic Genealogy*, developed the following Informed Consent Form. He asserts that this Informed Consent Form is NOT legal advice. **Neither Blaine Bettinger nor Kathy Lynne Marshall make any representation that these forms are legally binding or sufficient for their intended purpose.**

What follows is a sample Agreement the family genealogist may consider requesting family DNA testers sign before they submit their DNA test sample. It ensures the tester understands that DNA testing can reveal genetic surprises, like a biological sibling or parent they didn't know they had. If the tester doesn't want to handle their results themselves, the Informed Consent gives them the power to decide how they want their test results managed by the genealogist, or others. While the form may provide a safety net for the tester and help the genealogist decide whether to reveal potentially difficult revelations from the DNA results, it is not mandatory the tester sign such a form.

Informed Consent Agreement

Thank you! You've agreed to provide a DNA sample to a genetic genealogy testing company. After you mail out your DNA sample (either a cheek swab or a saliva collection), the company will analyze some of your DNA and will provide your admixture estimates ("ethnicity") and a list of your genetic matches in the database. Your matches will be able to see you as one of their matches.

I will provide you with access to your test results and will answer any questions you may have about your results. You may, at any time now or in the future, ask me to remove your DNA test results from the company database, to the extent possible.

If you'd like to keep your test results as private as possible (understanding that DNA is ultimately identifiable even when anonymous), upon request I can use an unidentifiable pseudonym and will not associate the results with an identifiable email address.

Please check ONLY one of the following options:
_____ I DO want to be able to access my DNA test results;
_____ I do NOT want to be able to access my DNA test results; OR
_____ I DO want a summary of my DNA test results.

Please check ONLY one of the following options:
_____ I DO want to assign an unidentifiable pseudonym to my DNA results; OR
_____ I DO want to use my real name with my DNA results.

Please check ONLY one of the following options:
_____ I DO want you to share with me any unexpected results from my DNA test; OR
_____ I do NOT want you to share with me any unexpected results from my DNA test.

Please check ONLY one of the following options:
_____ I do NOT grant permission to transfer my raw data or results to any other testing company;
_____ I DO grant permission to transfer my raw data or results to ANY other testing company; OR
_____ I DO grant permission to transfer my raw data or results ONLY to: _____

Please check ONLY one of the following options:
_____ I do NOT grant permission to use my raw DNA data for any third-party tool or database;
_____ I DO grant permission to use my raw DNA data for ANY third-party tool or database; OR
_____ I DO grant permission to use my raw DNA data ONLY for: _____

Please initial your understanding and agreement to the following:

_____ I have read The Genetic Genealogy Standards (www.geneticgenealogystandards.com).

_____ I understand that DNA testing can have unexpected results, including discovering that family members may not be biological family members and that I have close biological relatives that I did not previously know.

_____ I hereby grant you [_____] full access to my DNA test results, including my raw data, subject to my selections above. My signature below indicates my voluntary agreement to provide my DNA sample according to the selections above.

Name (Print): _____

Signed: _____ Date: _____

Which family members should do a DNA test?

Who in your family should be DNA tested to get the biggest bang for your buck? Testing the oldest generation is often the best course of action. The members of this generation might not be available to test in the future, so it's important to get a DNA sample with an older relative's permission as soon as possible. FamilyTreeMagazine.com can help you decide which family members to test and why. Fill in the spaces below with the family members you decided to DNA test.

- **Elders**: As many eldest elders as your pocketbook allows should be DNA tested *immediately* for all your family lines. Their DNA will have the greatest commonality with your ancestors who lived before 1900. Don't wait to test these precious resources, or you will regret it later.

Name and contact: _____

_____

Name and contact: _____

_____

Name and contact: _____

_____

Name and contact: _____

_____

Name and contact: _____

_____

Name and contact: _____

_____

- **Parents**: Testing your known biological parents is the best way to determine whether your DNA Matches are related to you on your maternal or paternal side. Their ethnicity results will also tell you which parts of your own ethnicity were inherited from each of them.

  Name and contact: _____

  _____

  Name and contact: _____

  _____

- **Spouse(s) or Partner(s)**: Testing your spouse(s) or baby-making partner(s) will reveal his or her ethnicity and find DNA Matches on their side which will be valuable information for your children-in-common.

  Name and contact: _____

  _____

  Name and contact: _____

  _____

- **Yourself**: Testing yourself makes it easier to find other relatives who match your DNA.

  Name and contact: _____

  _____

- **Full Siblings**: Testing known siblings who have your parents will shed light on the similarities and differences between you, since you didn't inherit exactly the same genetic material from your parents. Your sibling will yield some different DNA Matches from other relatives that you may not match because of the randomness of DNA distribution among siblings.

Name and contact: _____

_____

Name and contact: _____

_____

Name and contact: _____

_____

- **Half Siblings**: Testing known half siblings who share one of your parents helps determine the DNA segments you received from the parent you both have in common. Your sibling will yield DNA Matches for the parent you do not share.

Name and contact: _____

_____

Name and contact: _____

_____

Name and contact: _____

_____

Name and contact: _____

_____

- **First Cousins** (share a common grandparent): Testing cousins expands the reach of your known DNA matches. First cousin DNA will help you understand who your common grandparents were.

Name and contact: _____

_____

Name and contact: _____

_____

Name and contact: _____

_____

Name and contact: _____

_____

- **Second** cousins (share a common great-grandparent):

Name and contact: _____

_____

Name and contact: _____

_____

Name and contact: _____

_____

- **Third** cousins (share a common great-great-grandparent):

  Name and contact: _____

  _____

  Name and contact: _____

  _____

  Name and contact: _____

  _____

- **Adult Children**: Half of your adult children's DNA matches will not be a subset of your own matches since they inherit half their DNA from their other parent.

  Name and contact: _____

  _____

  Name and contact: _____

  _____

  Name and contact: _____

  _____

HINT: DNA companies offer significant sales on DNA test kits during holidays. *Buy several and give them as holiday presents. Each year, Kathy Marshall asks her sons to give her a Christmas present by getting themselves tested with another of the DNA companies*

Which DNA test should your family take? Each DNA testing company offers slightly different information and results. Here are a few considerations for the major companies, as of 2022.

Ancestry and MyHeritage

Ancestry.com and **MyHeritage.com** are the largest companies, the latter with 52 million family trees and the former with 100 million trees. Arguably, they offer the most comprehensive, and expensive, options for genealogical analysis.

Both offer autosomal DNA testing, which uses 22 of the 23 chromosomes every human receives from each parent. That type of genetic data can provide estimates of where in the world your ancestors came from and who is related to you.

Both companies have DNA tools, instructions, podcasts, and videos to help you further determine who your ancestors were. Ancestry and MyHeritage have photo enhancement software you can use to repair your old photographs.

Both companies allow you to store your family tree and use their services to find online documents about your relatives. Most people who purchase a DNA test only want to know what countries their ancestors came from. Genealogists want to go the extra mile and identify specific relatives in specific towns within specific countries.

MyHeritage offers a useful chromosome browser to help determine which chromosome segment people match on. Ancestry does not offer that desirable tool.

Here's a sample ethnicity map from MyHeritage.com. The colored areas indicate where Kathy's ancestors came from hundreds of years ago.

Kathy's Ethnicity map from MyHeritage.com

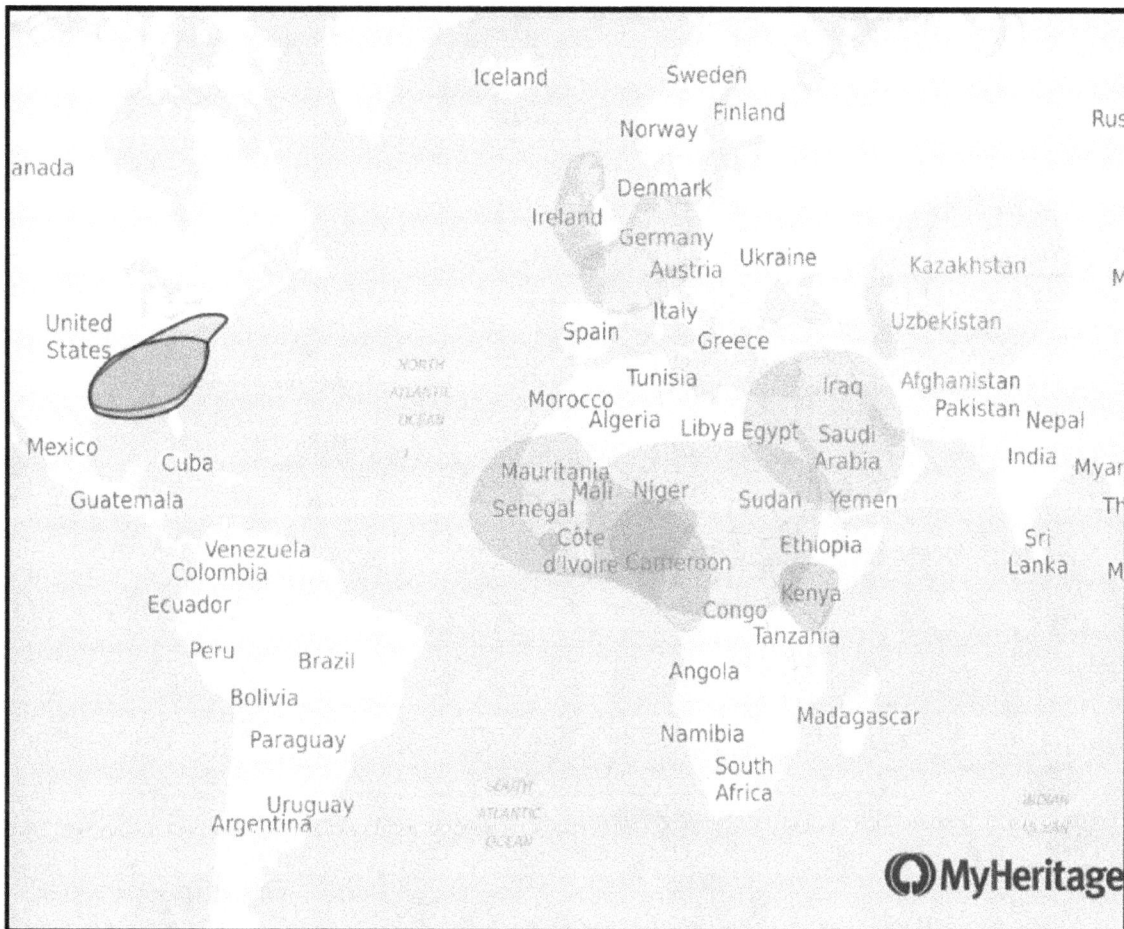

AFRICA

● **Nigerian**	24.5%
● **West African**	8.8%
● **Sierra Leonean**	8.2%
● **Kenyan**	3.9%
● **Central African**	1.7%

EUROPE

● **Irish, Scottish, and Welsh**	26.9%
● **North and West European**	23.2%

ASIA

● **Central Asian**	2.0%

MIDDLE EAST

● **Middle Eastern**	0.8%

Ancestry and MyHeritage also identify tens of thousands of relatives who match specific segments of your DNA. Genealogists crave this information. Here's an example of Kathy's matches from Ancestry.com.

Closest of Kathy Marshall's Paternal DNA Matches in ancestry.com

By parent **BETA**   **All matches**   By location

Filter by: ● Unviewed   ♗ Common ancestors   ✉ Messaged   📝 Notes   ⚥ Trees ∨   Shared DNA ∨

Reset filters

Close Family

Michal O███
1st cousin
565 cM | 8% shared DNA
Paternal side

⚥ Public linked tree
18,851 People
♗ Common ancestor

📝 ♥ Marshall side. ♥ Dooley side

Jocelyn███████
1st cousin
480 cM | 7% shared DNA
Paternal side

⚥ Public linked tree
4 People
♗ Common ancestor

A.H.
Managed by Alisha Hale
2nd – 3rd Cousin
314 cM | 5% shared DNA
Paternal side

⸬ Unlinked Tree

📝 Matches lwjwilson who may descend from Stephen marshall, Talbot, GA Myers? Crewetts? Matches KM, A.H., DonaldCurtisLucas, Desne, Judy Kim, K.K., K.C., eppersonpaul1, Lloyd Frazier, Dennis Rhodes, Lamont Helm, Christopher Reis. I already sent her 9 msgs. They just did the NA test for fun.

Owen ████████ IV
2nd – 3rd Cousin
252 cM | 4% shared DNA
Paternal side

⸬ Unlinked Tree

23andme and FamilyTreeDNA

The DNA testing companies 23andme and FamilyTreeDNA provide Y-DNA (paternity test) and mtDNA (mother's lineage) haplogroup reports on the 23rd chromosome we get from each of our parents. These tests track the migratory pattern of your father and mother's lineage from East Africa, where the first humans were found. As those ancestors ventured out of eastern Africa, they branched off in diverse groups that crossed and re-crossed the globe over tens of thousands of years. Some of their migrations can be traced through haplogroups (families of lineages that descend from a common ancestor). Your maternal haplogroup can reveal the migration patterns of women in your maternal line and it's a test that men and women can benefit from. 23andme showed that Kathy's B4a1a1a maternal haplogroup (and that of her brother, sister, mother, grandmother and so on) came from Madagascar, the fifth largest island in the world, which is located off the east coast of Africa.

A Y-DNA test–also known as a paternity test—is legally defensible. Although, for genealogical research, it is used to trace the migratory path followed by the men of your paternal line. This test is only for men. Kathy's brother, Greg, took the Y-DNA paternity test with 23andme and with FamilyTreeDNA. Both tests affirmed his PF-4088 haplogroup, which proved that his (and his siblings) paternal line came from Europe. Y-DNA testing also showed that a white man with the surname Marshall impregnated one of Greg's African female ancestors. This information opened up details about the Marshall lineage that led to the discovery of ancestors from the United Kingdom and Norway.

One caveat: 23andme does not offer a standard family tree format like other companies referenced here, but their system offers what they call an estimated tree. It shows, by generation, who your closest DNA matches are descended from. 23andme also offers health screening for select diseases, traits, and medical conditions.

Other DNA Testing Companies

There are smaller DNA testing companies that sell similar products, including: African Ancestry (mtDNA to find your African tribe); Living DNA (Autosomal, African/British/European ancestry); CRI Genetics (Ancestry, health, traits); Full Genomes, Veritas Genetics, Nebula Genomics, and Dante Labs, among others. The larger companies will probably have more potential DNA matches who share a common ancestor with you.

Other DNA Testing Sources

- Add books about DNA testing to your bookshelf. Kathy's favorites include: *The Family Tree Guide to DNA Testing and Genetic Genealogy* by Blaine T. Bettinger and *Genetic Genealogy in Practice* by Debbie Parker Wayne.
- AncestryDNA Learning Hub is free and managed by Ancestry.com.
- For a technical explanation of genealogy topics, try: isogg.org.
- Google DNA Podcasts to locate experts who speak about DNA testing.
- Meta/Facebook web pages from the major DNA testing companies provide a connection with other users and company representatives.

DNA Test Taken? Here are the Next Steps.

Establish a record of the family members who received their DNA test results. A sample DNA Consent Form follows. The genealogist will analyze the results and may be able to determine more generations of common ancestors. DNA doesn't lie. Awkward surprises may surface, like additional unexpected relatives that must be dealt with sensitively.

Which Family Members Took a DNA Test?

Compile a list of your relatives who have DNA tested and which tests they have taken. It's helpful to test on multiple platforms to find more relatives who might enlarge your proven family tree.

Tester Name	Ancestry	23and me	Family Tree DNA	My Heritage	Other (Name)

Step 6. Discuss Uneasy Topics with the Committee

Aside from the paranoid folks who think they will be cloned if they give a saliva sample to a DNA lab, most people love that DNA testing can estimate where in the world their family came from. DNA doesn't lie, though. It lays bare those family stories which stretch the truth to blur embarrassing or painful secrets. Award-winning author and genealogist, Bernice Bennett, has given several talks about the emotional side of DNA. She says, "DNA [testing] is just like a big roller coaster of emotions. People talk about being frustrated, overwhelmed, unable to think clearly and being speechless when they get their results. There's also sometimes denial that 'this just can't be true.' Some get so irritable they just can't deal with the unexpected heritage revealed by DNA data."

DNA results could reveal a previously unknown family member who was conceived from an extramarital affair, rape or incest, or who was given away in an adoption. But there are many other sensitive topics, rivalries, and differences in memory that often come up when people get together to talk, whether these issues come from DNA reveals, family stories, or genealogical research. Here are some uneasy family-oriented topics that easily come to mind:

A Pile of Potentially Sticky Issues

• Pa-Not-Pa (who's the daddy?)	• Many marriages	• STD, herpes, etc.
• Rape	• Prison record	• Scary medical condition like cancer
• Incest	• Drug abuse, alcoholism	• Death
• Prostitution	• Gambling addiction	• Suicide
• Infidelity	• Domestic violence	• Coming out sexually
• Adoption	• Slavery issues	• Depression
• Abortion	• Homelessness	• Murderer or victim

Understand and accept that you *will* uncover distressing events when dredging up dusty memories in families. But just because you uncovered juicy family secrets during your research, should you write about them in a memoir or family history book that lots of people will see? Should you be concerned about who might get hurt if you reveal those secrets? Should you tell the complete truth, only bits and pieces, or ignore the damaging factual information altogether?

Are your family dynamics prone to *throwing* the Thanksgiving Day turkey instead of eating in peaceful harmony? If so, discussing potential issues like mixed-race relatives and mis-attributed parentage (also known as Pa-not-Pa) before the family meeting may be helpful to quell those issues in advance. There are also certain ethical and legal ramifications to consider before you "tell the truth, the whole truth, and nothing but the truth," as Perry Mason used to say. The committee should discuss these potential stumbling blocks before finalizing plans for the Harambee.

What follows are some of the more common issues which might arise and some mitigations the committee might consider, to ensure your Family Harambee stays on a positive note.

What Do You Mean I'm Black?

Imagine the surprise of people who all their lives thought they were pure Caucasian White, but DNA results indicate they have a small percentage of African, East Indian, Asian, or Native American heritage. This happened to anti-Black Ku Klux Klan leader, David Duke, who learned on a national TV show that 14% of his DNA was from Sub-Saharan Africa! By America's one-drop rule, that means he's Black!

Think how disturbing it might be for staunch White Nationalists to receive a Howdy Cousin email from previously unknown Afro-American relatives found after a DNA test uncovered the truth of their actual lineage? What should the Harambee committee do with that information if they were entrusted to manage the family's DNA results? Should they tell the family they are mixed race? How would you bring up the genetic truth, especially if you know certain people disdain other ethnic or religious or sexual-orientation groups?

What tactic should the committee take to address these types of findings at the Harambee, especially if the genetic truth affects more than one person?

_____

_____

_____

_____

_____

_____

_____

_____

_____

_____

_____

_____

_____

_____

_____

_____

_____

_____

_____

_____

_____

_____

_____

_____

_____

How Much White (Black, Native American, or Asian) Ancestry Do You Have?

While DNA testing is immensely useful in genealogy, it is also a prime trigger that can bring long-held secrets to life. In a study published in *The American Journal of Human Genetics* in December 2014, researchers used the ancestry data compiled by the commercial genetic testing company 23andMe to measure the percentage of African ancestry of people who self-identified as White. In South Carolina and Louisiana, researchers found that one in 20 people who called themselves White had at least two percent African ancestry. And in a lot of the South, about 10 percent of people who identified as White turned out to have African DNA. How is that possible and what does it mean? Simple. Human beings make babies, whether they are made consensually. The One Drop Rule established during slavery—one drop of Black blood makes you a Black person—could disrupt their entire outlook on life.

One of many reasons Afro-American genealogy is so difficult is because about 90% of Black folk living in the United States of America were enslaved forced workers at some point in their lives. They were regarded as property, like a cow or a plow, to enlarge their master's economic status. Such chattel property was usually not mentioned by name in birth or death certificates, Census records, or most other genealogy documents prior to 1865.

Further, the White master, or overseer, or master's friends and family, could usually demand sex from enslaved and free women whenever they wanted it. That resulted in a White man who isn't usually identified as the father of his mixed-race mulatto children on legal documents. And yes, rarely, the mixed-race couple was a Black man with a White woman.

Studies estimate that, on average, Black people in America have 20% Caucasian DNA because of forced race-mixing during the era of slavery. Kathy's DNA results revealed her heritage to be nearly 50% African and 50% European. Her family knew of no White people who had married into any of her family lines, yet a look in the mirror, backed up by DNA evidence, tells the tale of how many Whites must have commingled with Kathy's enslaved African ancestors during the period of slavery in America from 1619 to 1865.

What if the DNA or Ancestral Research Uncovers Jewish Ancestry?

"No, that can't be true," you might say. "My family has always been devout Catholics." Or maybe your family is Baptist, or Latter-Day Saints, or Methodist, or Muslim, or atheist. Guess what? The FamilyTreeDNA and 23andme companies use Y-DNA and mtDNA testing, which can detect genetic commonalities to Ashkenazi Jews who migrated to southern Europe from Israel and Judah before that. (aish.com) If this finding of Ashkenazi Jewish DNA is found, should the committee share that genetic truth with the test taker and the Harambee?

What if your family has a proud Jewish heritage? How would they react to proof your ancestors came from Prussia–now called Germany–and were card carrying Nazis? Should that be brought up in the Family Harambee?

_____

_____

_____

What other touchy subjects or family stories do you think might surface in your Family Harambee?

_____

_____

_____

_____

Step 7. Collect Family Genealogy Data

In order to identify potential upsetting subjects, one must know enough about the lineage. Ideally, there's already a genealogist in the family who has already been collecting family information. There's usually one person in each family who has the burning desire to bring ancestral stories to light. In Kathy's experience, very few genealogists get around to putting their research into a format that others can read and understand, let alone be interested in. Often, these passionate souls work in a vacuum, squirreling away documents in boxes and binders, like nuts hidden in the ground for winter.

This workbook encourages genealogists to share their ancestral findings with others. They must engage with other people, provide the family with generational family data, stories, photographs, and DNA results. If presented correctly, the information will be so interesting to others they will want to jump on the bandwagon to learn more. Some people have unique talents for handling situations that can cause flare-ups during family gatherings. Offering to involve everyone in the history gathering process may soften the issues that can rupture harmony.

What follows is a sample letter containing three pages of forms that could be sent via email or snail mail to each family to fill out and return to the committee. Change the wording as you see fit. The data will help the genealogist and committee flesh out the family lineage.

NOTE: A variety of data collection forms are available online, like from the free National Genealogy Society's Genealogy Forms, as well as from the for-fee genealogy companies listed in Step 5.

Sample Letter Transmitting Family Report Forms
Before the Harambee

Greetings family,   Date_____

It's been a long time since we got together and chatted about old times. A few of us are interested in getting together soon for a Family Harambee to learn more about our ancestors and their contributions. (Harambee means all pull together in Kiswahili, Kenya's national language.) How about meeting next (month)_____ (year) _____?

To prepare, we are gathering our family history to prepare a booklet. Our family genealogist, (name)_____, has already made some exciting discoveries we will share at the Harambee, but first, we need more information about your family.

With your help, our effort will be a success. Please print out the attached three-page Family Data Sheet, fill in the pages as completely as you can, and email or snail mail it back to me by (date)_____. Our genealogist needs correct information to update the family tree.

Please attach any photographs of your family members to include in our online family tree and in the pamphlet we plan to prepare for the family's use.

We look forward to receiving your completed forms by (date)_____.
Please contact me if you have questions or if you want to volunteer and help the committee make the Harambee a fabulous event to remember.

Sincerely,

Name: _____

Phone: _____

Committee email address: _____

Committee mailing address: _____

_____

Family Records Sheet 1 (Partner/Spouse)

Prepared by _____ Phone: _____

Partner1/Spouse1: _____

Born date: _____

Married date:_____

Died: _____

Father:_____

Mother:_____

Partner2/Spouse2: _____

Born date: _____

Married date:_____

Died: _____

Father:_____

Mother:_____

Partner3/Spouse3: _____

Born date: _____

Married date:_____

Died: _____

Father:_____

Mother:_____

(Print out more sheets for additional partners/spouses in this family)

Family Records Sheet 2 (Children)

Prepared by _____ Phone: _____

Full Child's Name	Born When & Where?	Died When & Where?	Married to Name	Married When & Where?

From our esteemed elders to the tiniest baby, we would love to include photographs of your family, in the family tree and genealogy book we plan to produce from the Harambee. Use your smartphone to take excellent pictures of the old photographs and email them to the committee address below. Don't forget to label the photo file names with the people in the photo, approximate original photo date, and location when the picture was taken.

Family Records Sheet 3 (Stories)

Prepared by _____ Phone: _____

It's story time! Please consider emailing some of your family stories that others might like to hear, like fun memories, sad memories, beautiful memories, scary memories. Be sure to indicate the date and place the memories occurred, and the names of family members involved. Better still, interview your direct-line elders now. Be careful though! People might clam up if you start by asking questions that are too personal. Ease into the interview.

You could purchase a memoir journal with a variety of simple questions you might ask. Or try 50+ Conversation Starters for Awkward Family Gatherings. Start here:

- What is your earliest memory?
- Where did you grow up?
- Describe your school life.
- What were your parents like?
- Who were your childhood friends and what did you like to do with them?
- How did you meet your first boyfriend, girlfriend, or spouse?
- What is something you got away with as a child your family doesn't know about?
- What has been the happiest day of your life so far, and why?

You can type the stories on a computer or dictate them on your smartphone using a voice memo app. Be sure to label the stories with the names of the people interviewed, when and where they were recorded.

If you have questions about this, free to ask our genealogist for help
(name_____ phone: _____).

Please return the completed forms, and the stories if you have any, and mail them by
(date)_____ to:

Name: _____

Phone: _____

Committee email address: _____

Committee mailing address: _____

_____

Step 8. Develop Family Tree and Charts

Charts that clearly show how family members are related to one another may be helpful in understanding their relationships. Include as many family members into a single family tree as possible, building the tree three ways:

- **UP** (meaning, back in time) from the focus person, e.g., current head of household, to include deceased ancestors. In the following examples, the author, Kathy Marshall, is the focus person in the following charts, so her parents, siblings, and children are listed.
- **DOWN** to include the focus person's direct descendants (children, children's children, etc.) to the present day.
- **WIDE** to include the siblings for each generation.

The more accurate and inclusive your family tree is, the more likely that DNA testing can identify additional relatives. If this is the case, you will find documented lineage that can help your search for ancestors.

There are various genealogy companies, like the free FamilySearch, or for-fee Ancestry, MyHeritage, and FamilyTreeDNA (and others) who allow you to enter your information into an online family tree and print various charts and show familial relationships.

Genealogy Explained provides an online list of the Best Genealogy Software, but there are many others to consider for your needs. Google "family tree chart makers" or "family tree charts" for some examples.

Four common family tree charts are: Pedigree, Family Tree, Family Group, and Fan charts. There's also a Common Ancestor chart Kathy developed for her family members to see how they connect to a common ancestor.

Sample Pedigree Chart

This Pedigree chart from FamilyTreeDNA shows three generations of Kathy Marshall's direct-line ancestors. If there was more space, Kathy's name would be listed to the left of her father, Thomas Richard Marshall. Her grandparents are in the center column, and her eight great-grandparents are in the right column.

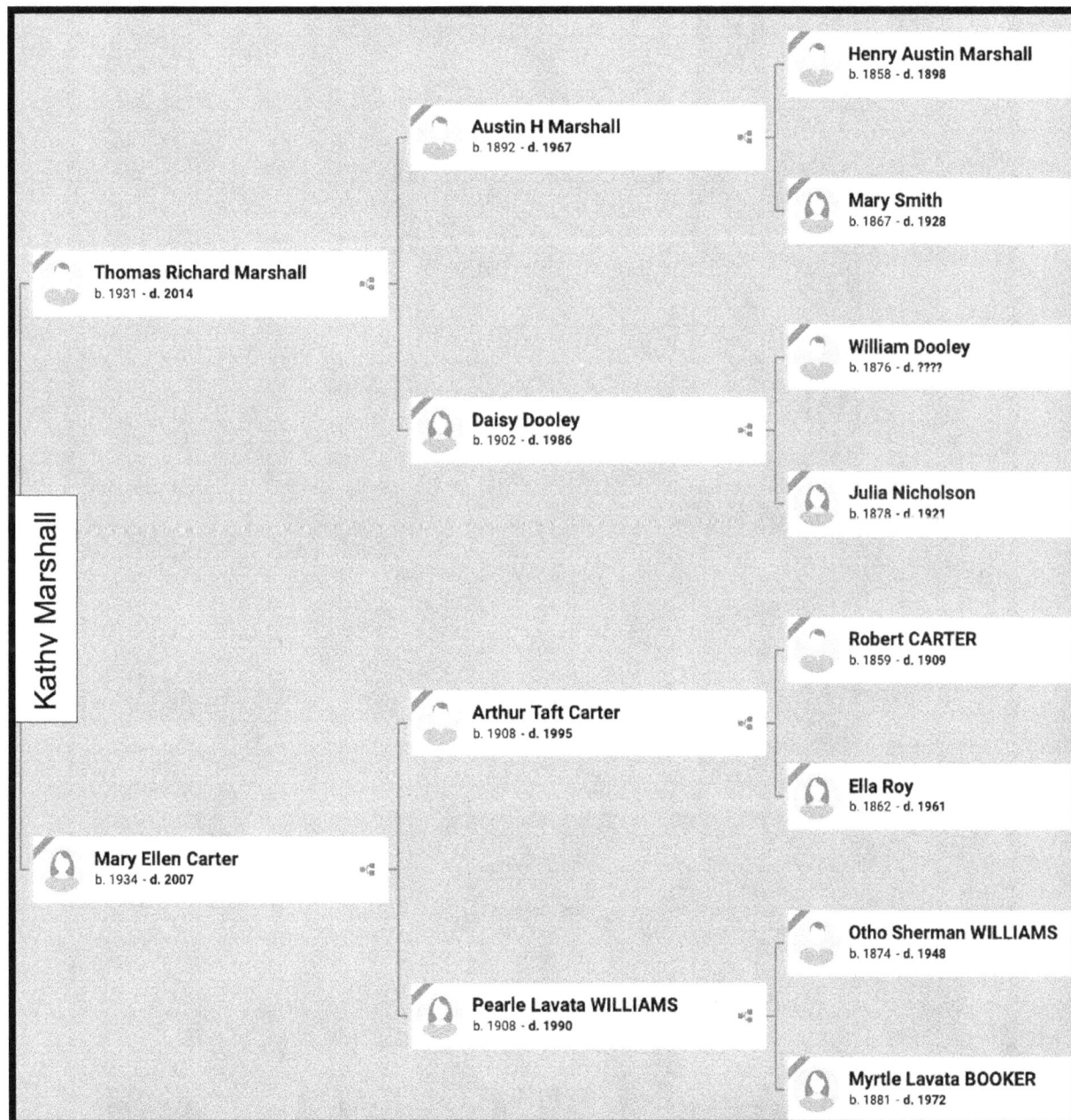

Sample Family Tree

This Family chart shows Kathy's ancestors (UP) and siblings (WIDE) and descendants (DOWN). This chart is from Ancestry.com.

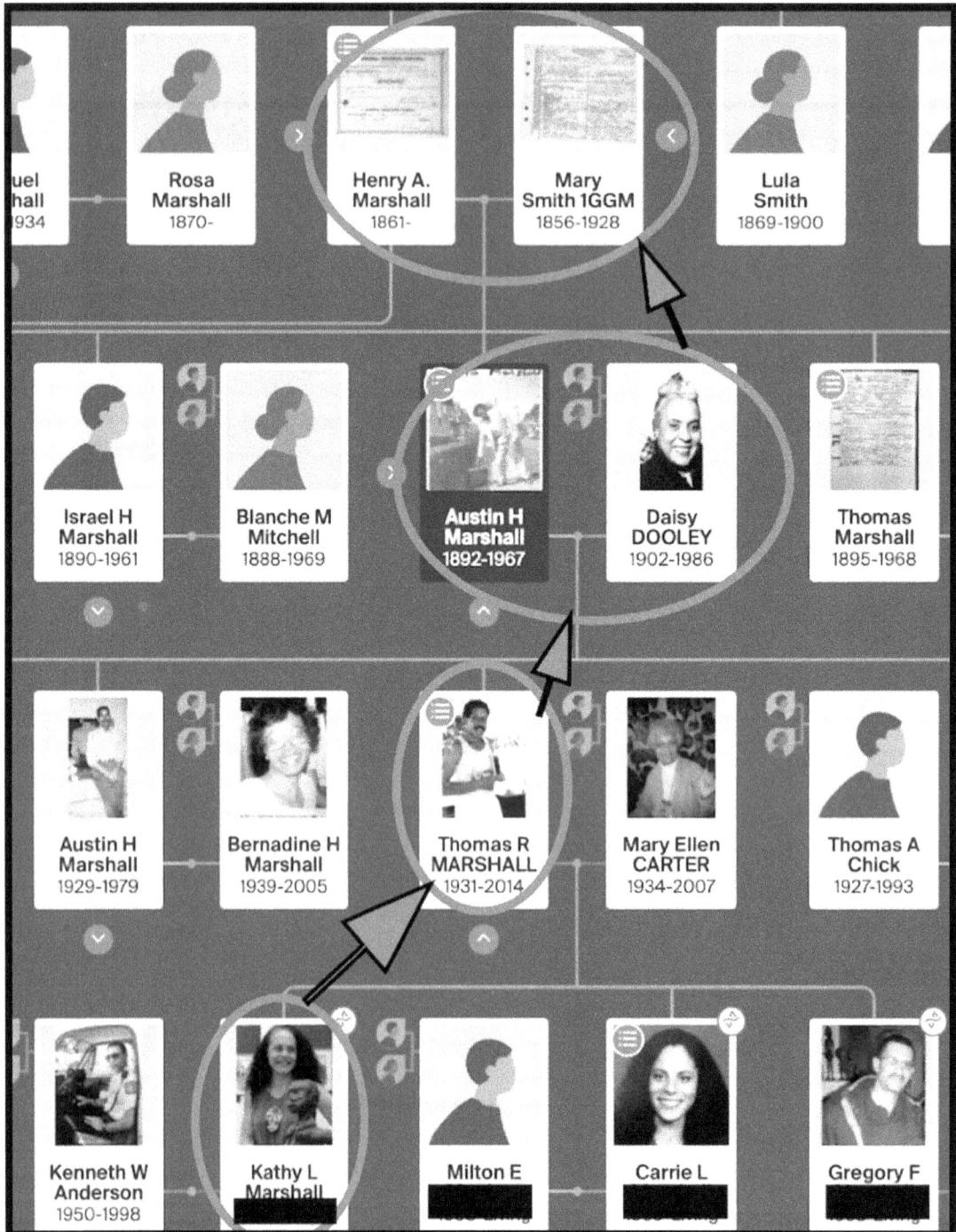

Sample Family Group Sheet

This chart lists the parents and children of the two focus people who are Kathy Marshall's great-grandparents, Henry A. Marshall and Mary Smith. This chart came from Ancestry.com.

Family group sheet

Husband Parents

Samuel Marshall 2GGF
1830 - 1880

Emeline E E Bunkley
1835 -

Wife Parents

Israel Smith 2GGF
1833 - 1901

Laura Ligon 2GGM
1840 - 1926

Husband　　　　**Alternate Spouses (2)**　　**Wife**　　　　**+ Add another spouse**

`1 ANCESTRY HINTS`

Henry A. Marshall 1GGF?
BIRTH: abt 1861 in abt Talbot, GA
DEATH: Deceased

Profile　　Search　　Edit

`1 ANCESTRY HINTS`

Mary Smith 1GGM
BIRTH: Abt 1856 in Alabama, USA
DEATH: 15 Aug 1928 in Muscogee County, Georgia, USA

Profile　　Search　　Edit　　Focus

Relationship Events

Marriage

14 Nov 1888 in Muscogee, Georgia, USA

Children　　　　　　　　　　　　　　　　　　　　　　**+ Add a child**

Clifford Marshall Son	BIRTH 20 Sep 1890 in Columbus, Georgia	DEATH 1 Aug 1964 in 8115 Cedar, Cleveland, Cuyahoga, Ohio, USA	1 Hint
Israel H Marshall Son	BIRTH 09 Nov 1890 in Columbus, Muscogee, Georgia	DEATH 27 MAR 1961 in Cleveland,Cuyahoga,Ohio	1 Hint
Austin Henry Marshall Sr. Son	BIRTH 19 Sep 1892 in Columbus City, Muscogee, Georgia	DEATH 23 Nov 1967 in Columbus City, Muscogee, Georgia	3 Hints
Thomas Marshall Son	BIRTH 21 Jul 1895 in Columbus, Muscogee, Georgia	DEATH 16 Mar 1968 in Phs MT Sinai Medical Center	1 Hint
Cora Lee Marshall Daughter	BIRTH 06 Dec 1898 in Muscogee, Georgia	DEATH 26 Feb 1919 in Columbus, Muscogee, Georgia, United States of America	1 Hint

Sample Family FAN Chart

This FAN Chart from FamilySearch.org color codes Kathy's familial relationships.

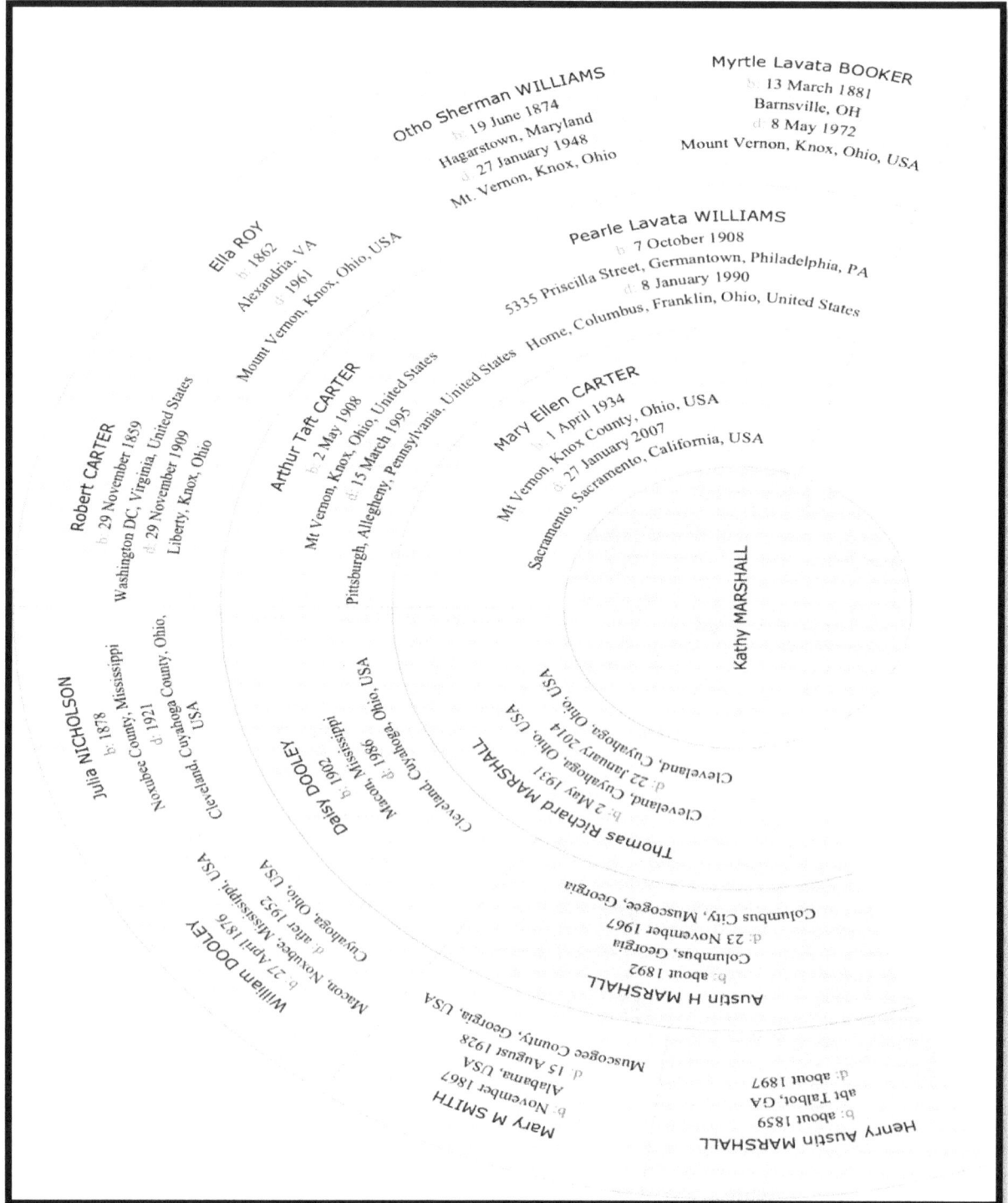

Common Ancestor Chart

This chart makes it easy for living people (bottom row) to see how they relate to a common ancestor in the top row: Robert Marshall (1642-1698, England).

Common Ancestor: Robert Marshall Sr. (1642-1698, Bedfordshire, England)

Generation	Line to EDDIE / Tony & Jennifer K	Line to KATHY / AZMINA	Line to AMY / JP	Line to ERIKA
1	John Joseph? Marshall & Sarah Malone (1661?-1728)	John Joseph? Marshall & Sarah Malone (1661?-1728)	John Marshall & Sarah Malone (1695?-1733, Isle of Wight to Brunswick, VA)	John Marshall & Sarah Malone (1695-1733, Isle of Wight to Brunswick, VA)
2	Capt John Marshall & Mary Malone (1725-1782)	Capt John Marshall & Mary Malone? (1725-1782)	Capt John Marshall & Mary Malone (1725-1782)	Capt John Marshall & Mary Malone (1725-1782)
3	Benjamin Marshall Sr. (1745-1818, TN)	David G. Marshall? (1740-1784, Halifax, NC)	David G. Marshall (1740-1784, Halifax, NC). Amy's 6xGGF	David G. Marshall (1740-1784, Halifax, NC)
4	Samuel Marshall (1785-1857)	Stephen B. Marshall? (1767-1831, Putnam) & Slave Hannah? (1781)	Lucy Marshall (1758-1829) & William Blount 1755-1825)	Stephen B. Marshall (1767,NC-1831,GA)
5	2x Jesse W. Marshall (1809 NC-1895, GA)	**[boxed]** William B. Marshall (1796) or Slave Sam (1813) or Jesse Marshall (1809)?	Richard Blount (1790-1841) & Ruth	William B. Marshall (1796-1874) & Rosa Marshall
6	1x Alfred A. Marshall (1846-1922, GA)	**[boxed]** 2x Samuel Marshall (1830-?) & Mary Wilkinson or Emeline Bunkley	William Blount (1823,GA-1884,TX) & Martha (1823-1870)	Albert Marshall & Clara Marshall
7	Hewey L. Marshall (1902-1963)	1x Henry A. Marshall (or Austin Marshall)? & Mary Smith	Oliver Marshall Blount (1857,GA-1924,TX) Emma(1865-1900,TX)	Mariah Marshall & John Walton
8	Jerry D. Marshall	Austin H. Marshall & Daisy Dooley	John F. Blount (1888-1969, TX) & Dora (1897-1981)	Walker Carter & Amelia Walton
9	Private	Thomas Marshall & Mary Carter	Emma Blount & John Lyles	Private
Living	EDDIE — Y-DNA to Greg 110/111; Tony & Jennifer K from Benjamin Marshall	KATHY, Greg, Carrie, Pershell, Austin, Jocelyn, Lori, Michal, Carolyn, Matthew; AZMINA, 11 cM to KM	AMY — 4.1 cM to KM; JP & Nancy descend from Matthew Marshall and Rhoda	ERIKA — 6.9 cM to KM

59

Step 9. Organize the Family Data

Have you been throwing your family's birth, death, census, probate and land deeds records into a box, or into file folders, or three-ring binders, or on a computer? That level of disorganization makes it impossible to figure out the family history.

Many experts agree that whether you use a binder, folders, a notebook, or a computer to organize your genealogy documents, alphabetize the files by surname so you can quickly find the family you want to research. Within each surname folder or binder, file items in chronological order, starting with the individuals' birth and ending with their death.

Kathy Marshall prefers to sort all documents by family surname using one large three-ring binder for each family line, then by each person within that family surname. Each person should have a separate file folder of genealogy documents that pertain to them. Sort the person documents by newest date (i.e., death) listed on top and the oldest—birth records—on the bottom or back of the file. In line with various Genealogy Gurus, like Dr. Shelley Murphy, Kathy creates a timeline of events for each person from the collected documents. A spreadsheet works well for this exercise, with columns labeled: "Name, Year, Age, State, City, Event, Citation, and Notes/Questions."

Enter pertinent information from each collected document into the spreadsheet, then sorted by Year or Name, or other field, as desired. A printed timeline is affixed to the front of each person's file. The following example is a timeline of Kathy's Grandmother Daisy, and her parents and grandparents. Spreadsheets make it easy to sort the family information to clarify who was where and when.

Sample Timeline

FINDING DAISY: FROM THE DEEP SOUTH TO THE PROMISED LAND

B=Birth, D=Death, M=marriage, W=Will/Deed, C=Census, DI=divorce, L=owned Land
Goal: Document events from Daisy's obituary. Why did she lie about being born in Noxubee, MS?

Name	Year	Age	State	City	County	Event	Resource Citation	Notes / Questions
Daisy Dooley	1902	0	MS	Macon	Noxubee	Birth	Cuyahoga Marriage Records	
Daisy Dooley	1905	3	MS	Macon		Birth sister Ruby		
Daisy Dooley	1910	8	MS	Macon	Noxubee	Residence	1910 Census, Beat 3	7, 1903, MS, Nox, Mu, F, daughter, single, Wm Dooley, MS, Julia Dooley, MS, schoolY, household: Wm, Julia, Willie Lee, Williams Dooley Jr., Rubie Lee, Henry Bell?, Steven P. McDonald?
Lovenia Dooley	1911	74	MS	Macon	Noxubee	Daisy's Grandmother Lovenia Dooley died?	1922 OH Marriage record for William Dooley & Emma Andersons	Maiden name Lavenia Olmster
Daisy Dooley	1914	12	MS	Macon	Noxubee	In School	Educable Children, Noxubee, MS	
Fannie C.N.Clayton	1915?	56	TN?	Memphis?	Shelby	Daisy's Grandma Fannie C.N.Clayton died?	Shelby, TN, Cert of Death	Sarcoma of femur?
Daisy Dooley	1916	14	MS	Macon	Noxubee	In School	Educable Children, Noxubee, MS	
William Dooley	1919	41	MO	St. Louis	St. Louis	Working in freight house in East St. Louis, living at __ C Street in St. Louis, MO	Military record	Working in freight house in East St. Louis, living at __ C Street in St. Louis, MO

If you are a computer aficionado, create a folder on your hard drive (or cloud space) with the family surname as the primary folder title, e.g., MARSHALL. If desired, take photos of printed documents and upload them into the computer folder. Or copy digital documents that are already online and paste them into the correct computer folder. Online files could be titled with the surname, firstname_year_document title, e.g., MARSHALL_ThomasR_2014_DeathCertificate.

Digital images of these documents may be input into an online family tree or stored on a personal computer or, less desirable, in a handwritten notebook.

Step 10. Research the Selected Family Member or Line

After receiving data from descendants of a selected family line, the genealogist should attempt to process the stories and photographs from relatives. To validate that family data, the genealogist should collect census records: birth, marriage, and death certificates; cemetery records; probate and land records; DNA testing results, etc. The goal is to piece together the daily lives of their ancestors from as many sources as possible and share that information at the Harambee, preferably in a book or binder.

There are many ways to present the research results to family members. Kathy's maternal family had a Designated Genealogist, meaning, *designated* by the elders as the family historian in the summer of 1982. Lavata Williams exceeded expectations. She took a genealogy course to determine what data was needed, mailed a form similar to the one in Step 7 to all family units, reserved Mohican State Park in Ohio for three days, and required families to pay room and meal fees in advance. She assembled the family data, stories from the elders, census and vital records, and typed all into a 22-page booklet in 1983. She revised it in 2003 for a second reunion to include photographs. Each family received a 31-page booklet for their records with pages similar to this excerpt from Genealogies: Myers, Williams, Booker, by M. Lavata Williams, 2003.

Mary Ellen (Carter) Marshall

Born: April 1, 1934; Mt. Vernon, Ohio   Died:

Married: Dr. Thomas R. Marshall, May 7, 1955, Columbus, Ohio

         Born: May 2, 1931; Cleveland, Ohio   Died

Children: Kathy Lynne, Carrie Lauren, Gregory Forest

Schooling: Mt. Vernon High School, Mt. Vernon, Ohio 1952; Sacramento City College 1966 University- Sacramento 1969 BA; California State University-Sacramento 1975 M

George William Carter

Born: February 22, 1936; Mt. Vernon, Ohio   Died: May 20, 2003;

Married: Tommie Jean Driskell, July 10, 1962; Grandville, Ohio

         Born: September 19, 1933; Grandville, Ohio   Died: Year 1999

Children: George William Jr., Tommy Gean Jr., Pamula Sue, Michael Lee

Schooling: Attended Mt. Vernon High School

Military Service: Air Force veteran; 1955-1961

Step 11. Create Family Email & Text Groups

The committee should create family email and telephone text groups containing the contact information of family members they wish to invite to gatherings, video chats, and social media pages. Additionally, if there are emergencies or changes in the Family Harambee itinerary, everyone would have access to this contact information. This information should be included in a Family Directory, along with the family data gathered in Step 7, and passed out at the Family Harambee so all participants have access to the same information. If yours is a large event, this will keep everyone abreast of the latest news. Here's a sample group email message.

Sample Family Group Email and Text Test Message

Dear family,

Several of our name_____ family members have formed a small committee to get ready for the next family gathering. Our genealogist,

name_____, has been working overtime to find out more about our name_____ history. I have added you to an email group to let you know about upcoming family events and our new social media accounts.

Please reply if you received this group email.

Many thanks!

Family Harambee Committee

Phone: _____

Email: _____

Mailing Address: _____

Permission to reproduce.

Step 12. Select a Family Harambee Date and Location

Selecting a date depends on whether the gathering will be a full-blown family reunion with hundreds of people, or small dinners with cousins during a genealogy trip, or a monthly Zoom session with relatives from all over America to chat about newly found information.

If it's a large Harambee, allow several months of lead time for people to plan to attend. The committee could survey family members on their preferred dates, places, and topics, then select the most convenient time.

An easier method is to let the committee select the date and location and simply notify the others of the decision.

Things to keep in mind are families who have children in school, people who work during the week, church obligations, and the availability of various locations for in-person meetings, etc. Here's an opportunity for the planning community to select their preferred Harambee date.

Committee Member Name: _____

Rank Possible Family Harambee gathering dates (#1 is your favorite date):

1. _____

2. _____

3. _____

4. _____

Select a Convenient Location for the Harambee

Solicit ideas on a meeting location from the committee. Consider whether the gathering will be best accommodated in a restaurant, park, family home, or a hotel with amenities like meeting rooms.

For small Harambee gatherings—less than a dozen family members—it would be easier to pick a date and a location and invite people to show up at the assigned time and place, instead of reserving rooms at a hotel and hoping family members pay their room reservations and show up as planned.

Otherwise, the committee should seek the recommendations of people who live in the area. Selecting a meeting location near where the ancestors lived makes it easier to visit the family homesite, cemeteries, libraries, and historical centers which could provide more information or photo opportunities.

Committee Member Name: _____

Rank Potential Gathering locations (#1 is your favorite location):

1. _____

2. _____

3. _____

4. _____

Step 13. Develop a Schedule of Events Itinerary

Post the itinerary on the private social media page, website, or blog and email the itinerary to participants in advance. Here is a partial example from Kathy's genealogy trip, followed by a blank itinerary you may use for your planning purposes:

Sample Itinerary

Date	Where Activity	Open/Time	Address	Phone	Notes
May 23	Delta 783 Sac to Atlanta	7AM takeoff	SMF, 6900 Airport Bl, Sac, CA		
May 23	Pickup Dollar Rental Car	3:15 PM	2300 Rental Pkwy, COllege Park, GA		
May 23	Meet Eddie at Holiday Inn	5 PM	520 John B. Wilson Ct, Lawrenceville, GA		
May 24	Meet/lunch with J. Marshall	11:00 AM	104 C. St., Eatonton, GA		
May 25	Talbotton Courthouse Vault	9:30 PM	26 S. Washington, Talbotton, GA		
May 26	Visit with M. Buckner	1-4PM	F. Mill Rd, J.City, GA		
May 27	St. James AME Church	10 AM	1002 6th Ave., Columbus, GA		
May 28	Bone Fish restaurant w/ cousins	2 PM	6763 Veterans Parkway, Columbus GA		

Blank Itinerary

Date	Where Activity	Open/Time	Address	Phone	Notes

Permission to reproduce.

Step 14. Committee Gets Ready for the Harambee

This step contains sample plans for a Harambee that will last a whole day, with a master of ceremonies and two-to-four speakers. Change whatever you wish if your event is shorter, say lasting a couple of hours at a restaurant. The primary aim is to be prepared in advance for conversations that might become tense with the divulging of difficult topics with a variety of attendees.

Discuss the Historical Facts the Genealogist Found

The genealogist should discuss with committee members the cultural coordinator the exciting and perhaps disturbing discoveries made from their genealogical research. This could include a slideshow containing easy-to-read charts or graphs or interesting stories developed from the facts. Step 8 has many examples of charts that may be presented in a PowerPoint-type slideshow presentation or in booklets given to each family. Examples of positive results are:

- Finding the parents of the focus person (explained in Step 3) for the focus family line being studied. Being able to trace the family lineage one generation back is indeed a cause for joy, especially regarding an adoption situation, or when the family name was shortened from the original family name in the Old Country on the way to America.

- Finding who the family's slaveholder was can open up a plethora of new information, such as where the owner's enslaved lived, who were part of the enslaved family unit, what type of work the enslaved did, their age, their complexion, and the dreaded knowledge of how much they were worth monetarily. While on the surface, that sounds like bad news to find proof your ancestors were chattel property, it is often the only way to learn anything about an enslaved person, so it becomes cherished information.

- Learning about the types of work the ancestors did. For example, in Kathy Marshall's *Finding Otho: The Search for Our Enslaved Ancestors*, she partially validated her family's belief that each generation in her family received their metalworking abilities from their enslaved ancestors. She is a welder, and each generation in her mother's maternal line has multiple people who worked with metal in some form or another. A manumission record showed one of Kathy's direct ancestors was freed in 1812 by the Antietam Ironworks in Maryland! That one document led to a score of additional records that proved her ancestor bought land and property, as well as who he married and who his children were. That was Kathy's first genuine success at finding evidence of her enslaved family and explains why *Finding Otho* is chock-full of interesting tidbits on how she finally broke through the 1870 brick wall to find answers, and how others can have the same success.

- Finding proof that a relative who fought in the American Revolutionary War can lead a present-day family becoming part of the Daughters of the American Revolution or the Sons of the American Revolution.

Discuss Troublesome Landmines the Genealogist Found

On the flip side, sensitive issues might be found under the dust by genealogical research. The genealogist and other committee members should work closely with the cultural coordinator before the Family Harambee to discuss the joyful and hurtful issues that might come out during the meeting. They should agree in advance how they will deal with the following sample issues that may surface:

A. **Who's the Baby Daddy?** Non-parental events (NPEs) where DNA or other evidence proves the daddy or mommy isn't who people think they are. This is easy to spot in a DNA match list where you would expect a child to have received about 3400 centimorgans (cMs) from their mother and 3400 from their father. If that does not occur, the person managing the DNA results may not know whether all family members already know that isn't the biological child of one (or both) of the parents.

It is an ethical issue. Should the committee blatantly call up the test taker and their parents to present the truth, or should the committee ignore it or do more research to determine what the truth is? Because a large percentage of people who take a DNA test only want to know which countries their ancestors came from and don't really care who their DNA matches are. The genealogy team must decide what to do with the information.

Kathy ignored those NPE results for one of her cousins who was only concerned about how much African DNA she had, not whether the Daddy she loved beyond words, now deceased, wasn't her bio Dad. Kathy could determine who the real father was using the same DNA match list but mentioned nothing about it to the cousin. Step 6 discusses these issues in more depth.

To learn more about the ways a third party can bring up issues related to adoptions and NPEs, Kathy recommends watching the Relative Race TV show on the byuTV streaming network as four teams find healing, hope, and new beginnings as they race to find their long-lost relatives.

Of even more help is watching the helpful December 11, 2022, edition of the Genealogy Adventures podcast when they interview the production crew of Relative Race to find out how they approach families about their unknown relatives (the pertinent information starts around minute 25). Staff reveal the gentle techniques they used to handle the difficult situation of telling family members about relatives nobody knew existed.

How does the Committee feel a NPE issue should be handled?

_____

_____

_____

_____

_____

_____

_____

_____

B. **Not related to anyone in the family?** This could likely indicate the DNA tester was adopted. Perhaps that child's parents were both killed and a neighbor took them in and raised them. That was quite common in the African American community where lynchings, false imprisonment, runaway parent(s), and maternal deaths left many children functionally orphaned. The Black community stepped in, willingly, to take care of those children. Should the genealogist enter information about non-related persons in an online family tree, or make a comment about the non-blood status in the file, or should they stay quiet? Should the genealogist try to learn whether the child knows their true biological status?

How does the Committee feel this issue should be handled?

_____

_____

_____

_____

_____

_____

_____

_____

C. **Where's my brother?** What if a biological parent or sibling DOES show up in an adopted child's DNA match list? Is it the genealogist's job to tell the child who their true biological family is?

How does the Committee feel this issue should be handled?

_____

_____

_____

_____

_____

_____

_____

_____

_____

D. **How to deal with elders?** What if a really old elder has unexpected irregularities in their DNA (e.g., they are not blood related to anyone in the family)? Should the genealogist shatter decades of stories and family members the elder knew, or should the committee let sleeping dogs lie until the elder passes away? How does the Committee feel this issue should be handled?

_____

_____

_____

_____

_____

_____

_____

_____

_____

How Should Disruptive Outbursts Be Handled?

Even though the master of ceremonies and cultural coordinator will do their best to avoid bad blood or ill feelings, disruptive outbursts may arise. Sometimes a story being told differs from what people had always heard or believed growing up (like being raised White but actually descending form at least one Black ancestor).

The committee could install "spotters" throughout the meeting room. Spotters would watch the participants' expressions to see whether anyone appears overly angry or sad. Those watchers could sit next to agitated person, offering to help them get a drink or get some fresh air. Removing potentially disruptive individuals from the room well before emotions escalate, might be beneficial to the entire Harambee.

What are the committee's thoughts on dealing with Disruptive people?

_____

_____

_____

_____

_____

_____

_____

Role Play Uncomfortable Situations in Advance

A non-committee member should be brought into a practice session, pretending to be an angry family member who is causing trouble. The committee can test their response team to quell any violence. The cultural coordinator should practice calming techniques, using empathy and understanding how to de-escalate the trouble. The committee could prepare family members in advance to expect new information about the family. Some preventative measures could be:

- Including in the invitation-to-the-Harambee letter that some interesting and previously unknown information has come to light about the family. Set the stage that there will be plenty of opportunities to take a break in their bedroom, enjoy the pool or stroll through the peaceful gardens outside, maybe offer on-site deep breathing or yoga classes. Make the diversions sound positive and pleasant.
- Having the master of ceremonies explain at the beginning of the event that there may be stories that nobody has heard before, or that some long-held family lore might have a new twist on them considering new research.

The genealogy team will probably find potentially difficult situations from their research. Already stated examples are children whose parents aren't blood related, or White people who learn they are part-Black, or people who find they have cousins from slave owners or their enslaved, or people who have Ashkenazy Jewish ancestry. How should the committee practice mitigation techniques to be ready for possible outbursts?

_____

_____

_____

_____

What Other Activities Did the Committee Devise for the Harambee?

To help make the expense of a Harambee worthwhile, conferences, family reunions, and other similar events often offer a variety of side trips for participants to enjoy. For example, the Harambee could be held in the County where the focus family line lived. Side trips could include a visits to the plantation or houses where family lived, cemeteries where family was buried. The committee could charter a bus to visit to the historical society, courthouse, or local library to research information about the family. If relatives still live in the area, a small Harambee might be arranged in their house or backyard or a nearby park.

What other activities might the committee arrange for the day(s) after or before the Harambee?

_____

_____

_____

_____

_____

What Music Should Be Selected for the Harambee?

If desired, the committee could solicit playlists from teenage, middle-age, and elder group representatives to provide a play list of music that could be heard in the background during meals, after hours, etc. Name the songs.

Event	Song	Musical Group

Develop and Practice the Master of Ceremonies Opening Statement

A sample opening statement for the Master of Ceremonies follows.

> *Note: The following are only suggestions. Customize this sample speech and timeframes for your specific needs.*

Sample Master of Ceremonies Opening Speech (Begin at 9 AM)

Dear family,

Welcome one and all. Thank you for taking time out of your busy lives to join us. We know how difficult it can be to juggle work and home life. So, I am happy to see all your smiling faces. It has been too long since we've been together. We have an exciting Harambee event planned for you, as shown on the itinerary at each table. *Harambee means "all pull together" in Kiswahili, which is the East-African country, Kenya's, national language.* And let me tell you, several of us have pulled out all the stops to make this event one you will not soon forget. I'd like to acknowledge the planning committee and their efforts to bring us together today (clap).

Let's get some housekeeping tips out of the way before we get started.
- Bathrooms are that way (pointing) and the lunchroom is that way (pointing).

- Make sure you visit the check-in table now if you didn't already pick up:
    - Name tags for each member of your family. Please wear your name tag at all times so we can get to know each other better.
    - One meal ticket for each family member. You won't get fed without them.
    - One family heritage booklet per family unit.

- Please turn off the ringer on your phones now so we don't get disrupted during the speeches; and if you get a call, please exit the room to answer your phone.

- The older kids will be entertained at the pool, basketball court, and tennis court, while the younger children will be supervised in the _____ room. You should have been given the childcare coordinator's phone number and email when you signed your children in this morning. In case you didn't, here's the childcare coordinator's phone number: (_____) _____-_____.

- We are a good looking group of people, aren't we? (clap) We have secured the services of a photographer to record our pretty faces all day long at this event. They will take a group photograph at 5:15 PM after the last speaker, right before happy hour.

- Please take as many photos and videos as you like at this event. We'll want to put together a video later to commemorate our time together.

- If, for whatever your reason, you don't wish to be photographed during this event, please go to the table at the back wall right now, take one of the red "No Photo" stickers and place it on the upper left side of your chest (the master of ceremonies should demonstrate how to affix the red sticker). The photographer, who will take pictures throughout our event today, will blur out the faces of people who wear a red sticker, to maintain their privacy. Understand that we have no control over other people taking your picture.

Okay, let's get started. Today, we plan to share with you the discoveries our talented genealogist cousin, (name)_____, and their helpers (name)_____ have made on our behalf. I marvel at how they could wade through all of those family data sheets you so kindly returned to us. I know we all appreciate the hundreds of hours they spent hunched over heavy deed and marriage books in cramped courthouses and libraries in the places where our family lived hundreds of years ago. Let's give them some love right now for their dedication to our family (clap).

Now, this is important. We want everyone to have a good time and learn something new about our family lineage. Some information revealed today may differ a bit from what you have heard for years. We may find we have a diverse group of relatives who we didn't know about before. We hope everyone will listen to the speakers respectfully, raise our hands if we have a question, use our quiet inside voices when we speak, and enjoy ourselves. If something said disturbs you, please get up and take a break for a while, then come back when you are feeling better. Okay?

After the prayer, (name)_____ will sing my favorite song. Then the keynote speaker, our talented genealogist, will take the podium, followed by a question-and-answer session. We'll take a lunch break from 11:30 AM to 1:30 PM in the _____ room. At 1:30 PM, our quilters will show their handiwork and you can look through the family heritage binders as our storyteller(s) make us laugh, cry, and be proud of our resilience despite slavery and Jim Crow. But we can't be kept down, can we? No sir! Am I right? (clap).

Then at 2:30 PM, we'll have a conversation about some interesting results the DNA testing found. Report to this _____ room with your children at 5:15 PM for the professional group photo, after the last speaker. Don't be late. Following group picture time, is no host bar happy hour in the _____ room, then dinner from 6 PM to 8 PM in the _____ room. At 9 PM, after the children have gone to bed, we'll have adult-only story time back here in the _____ room.

(9:30 AM introduce the first speaker)

Let's give a warm welcome to our keynote speaker, our beloved family genealogist, (name)_____. They will regale us with stories about how they became interested in genealogy, what they did with our family history data, and how far back in history our family goes. They, along with (name)_____, compiled the family information and stories and photographs you all sent into a wonderful booklet. Please save this written legacy for your children.

I hope we will all be open-minded about the interesting stories that were found during this evacuation project, digging for clues, finding treasure troves and a few landmines. They worked hard to document our family_____ lineage and I know you will cherish their efforts as much as I do.

(11:30 AM, after the keynote speaker)

Wasn't that a marvelous accounting everyone? (clap) I can't believe how much the genealogy team could uncover with the family data you provided. Lunch service starts now in the _____ room, so grab your kids, make sure you take your meal tickets you should have received at the check-in table this morning, and enjoy your meals.

After lunch, come back to this room at 1:30 for another storyteller, the quilt display, and your chance to browse through the family lineage binders. At 2:30 PM, the DNA Coordinator will share what they found from the folks who offered to take DNA tests to see how far back in history we could go. See you after lunch.

(1:30 PM after lunch)

May I have your attention? I'd like to encourage you to look at our quilt exhibit by quilters (name)_____ and _____ on the back wall. Also, for your viewing pleasure, are several family lineage binders. Check them out and learn how you too can organize your family data, photographs, and stories for a legacy to your children. And for those who want to hear another fascinating family tale, come and sit up front. Let me introduce our storyteller, (name)_____, who is going to spin another thrilling yarn about our family history. (clap)

(2:30 PM for afternoon speaker)

Once again, everyone, may I have your attention. It's time to take your seats and get ready for pearls of wisdom from our DNA expert. They will let us know how they do what they do, how they used our DNA testing results, and what they found out about our way-back family. As always, leave the room for a break if the need arises. Ready? Let's give (name)_____ a hand (clap).

(5:15 PM for photographs)

Everybody–including children–should report to the _____ room at 5:15 PM sharp so the photographer can get group photographs. (Speak loudly) Did you hear that? Everybody, including your children, should report to this room no later than 5:15 PM for group photographs, and they'll take individual family photographs if you want them. You don't want to miss this opportunity because of "CP" time, do you? That's colored people's time for you youngsters who don't know the expression. It means don't be late. The photographer will not wait for late birds for the group photo.The photographer will charge you directly for any individual family pictures you want from them at $___ per photograph.

- Write your own opening statement for the Master of Ceremonies. You may consider having elders and youngsters speak, in addition to the genealogist. You may have clergy in attendance to start the meeting and bless the food. You may have authors or poets speak, musicians play a song, singers or artists come to the podium. But it's helpful to carefully plan what the program will be and practice it in advance (especially is technology is involved).

_____

_____

_____

_____

_____

_____

_____

_____

_____

_____

_____

_____

_____

_____

_____

Sample Master of Ceremonies Concluding Statement

(5:45 PM at the end of the Harambee)

We hope you enjoyed the day's festivities and learned a lot about our wonderful family. Let's give it up for everyone who helped make this event a success (clap).

Introduce all the volunteers by name _____ (clap).

What's next? In the next few weeks, the committee will send every family unit the meeting minutes from this Harambee, along with digital photographs and videos to attendees on the email listing. For those of you without email, we shall snail mail you the information.

You will all be invited to attend a Zoom session in a few weeks after this meeting to wrap up what we learned and answer any more questions you might have about our lineage. Then we may start planning the next Harambee.

Enjoy your dinner in the _____ room from 6 to 8 PM. Don't forget your meal tickets in your Family Packet from the reception table.

For those of you who are interested, a bunch of us grown folks, only, will meet at 9 PM in the room_____ to talk about grownup things and maybe have a beverage, so please leave your kids with the Children's Coordinator or a babysitter.

Do you have questions before we adjourn this meeting and get ready for dinner?

Step 15. Invite Relatives to the Event

Write a letter and email explaining the purpose for the Family Harambee. The letter would include the date, meeting place, approximate cost, instructions, deadline for reservations, the Schedule of Events itinerary, and the committee's contact information.

Will your Harambee be a large family reunion, a few hours at a restaurant with a dozen people, or a picnic in the park? Will you talk about a specific paternal or maternal family line? Did your ancestor own land or invent something? Will you tell stories about a famous relative, or did you have a relative who was a notorious pirate, fought in the American Revolution, or was related to royalty?

The next page contains a sample invitation letter you are welcome to change to suit your needs.

Artwork by Mary Marshall, with permission

Sample Letter Inviting Family to the Harambee

Dear family,   Date: _____

Our genealogist, (name) _____, has found some exciting family news thanks to years of research, and several relatives who took DNA tests. We are happy to invite you and your family to attend a Family Harambee gathering on date_____ at (location)_____.

The attached instructions provide more information about our get together: the agenda, costs, menu choices, and how to reserve your space. You are encouraged to make your own sleeping and transportation arrangements.

Please contact the Coordinator if you have questions.

We hope to see you and your family at the Harambee.

Sincerely,

Coordinator name: _____

Coordinator address: _____

Coordinator telephone: _____

Coordinator email: _____

Attachment (Schedule of Events from Step 13)

Step 16. Conduct the Family Harambee

There are many scenarios for how a family gathering should be conducted, depending on how many participants there are and the location.

For Medium-to-Large Coordinated Events

Here is a sample flow of events for a moderate-sized event at a hotel.

Day Before the Meeting:

- Arrive a day earlier than everybody else at the venue.
- Ensure all rooms, meeting times and door signs, meals are correctly reserved.
- Ensure server staff are prepared for your event.
- Communicate with all committee members to ensure their duties are on point.
- The master of ceremonies should practice the opening and closing speeches.
- The cultural coordinator and office staff should ensure the meeting room is set up as desired for the keynote speaker, enough chairs, tables for displaying quilts and family lineage binders. They should test the microphone and projection device to ensure they work properly.
- The committee office crew should ensure the check-in table will be set up outside the meeting room.

Day of the Meeting:

- The committee office crew set up the check-in table outside the meeting room. Name tags, lunch and dinner meal tickets, and one copy of the family lineage booklet should be inside a manila envelope for each family unit, sorted by family surname. The check-in crew should be ready to welcome attendees by 8:00 AM. They should also set out the Family Harambee signage to direct people exiting an elevator toward the check-in table.

- The committee office crew should ensure the meeting room has enough chairs for the number of adults attending. If there will also be tables in that room, ensure they have tablecloths, agendas, flowers, pads of paper, and writing implements.
- The child coordinator should be ready to sign-in children by 8:00 AM.
- Attendees should arrive in the meeting room by (time)_____.
- Master of Ceremonies delivers speech in Step 14.
- Storytellers act out a few stories as people are entering the room and getting situated before the meeting begins at (time)_____.
- The master of ceremonies begins the meeting at (time)_____.
- Prayer, if desired.
- Singer, if desired.
- The master of ceremonies introduces the genealogist, who delivers their message, maybe via a PowerPoint presentation.
- Lunch at (time)_____.
- Storytellers act out a few stories at (time)_____.
- Lively third speaker to keep people awake. Maybe the history games coordinator, prizes for correct responses, maybe a family history quilt show, or family history binders that people can walk around and look through.
- Break.
- Roundtable discussion of uncomfortable topics led by the cultural coordinator.
- Break for dinner.
- Adult storytelling in private rooms.

For Small Family Harambee Gatherings

Here's an example of a more intimate gathering, perhaps in a private room in a restaurant or at someone's home.

- Order the meals (if not already pre-ordered).
- The Master of Ceremonies welcomes attendees and describes the agenda.
- The first speaker tells some light family stories to get people in a good mood as they eat.
- There should be plenty of wine to help quell potential troublesome situations that might surface.
- Family history booklets may be passed out after the dishes are cleared.
- The second speaker could be the genealogist who adds documentary meat to family stories and maybe delves into sensitive topics. A question-and-answer period could follow.
- The Master of Ceremonies invites everyone to a future Zoom session to discuss more of the genealogist's findings and results of the Harambee.

Step 17. Zoom Meeting Followup

Send out an invitation to the email group for a Zoom session that would recap the larger gathering which some people may not have been able to attend.

The Zoom Coordinator should:

- Help people get into the Zoom session, realizing that many people are not computer- or Zoom-literate.
- Help attendees mute themselves and turn on their video so others can see them.
- Handle all technical issues.
- Assist the speaker in sharing their screen so attendees can follow the presentation.

The genealogist should prepare a presentation which contains:

- The story of their journey to find the family lineage.
- Photographs of places they traveled (former homes, courthouses, libraries, etc.).
- Slides which describe how they approached the research.
- How they compiled the Family Data sheets families sent in.
- What the online family tree looks like for that family line.
- Pedigree and other family charts.
- Examples of DNA results: maps of a few family members which shows where their families lived hundreds of years ago.
- Examples of what the DNA match lists look like with a brief explanation of how to interpret how close the family relationship is to the test taker.
- Examples of some of the DNA analysis tools which help the genealogist determine who is related to whom.
- A Common Ancestor chart to give people an idea of how they may be linked to an ancestor who lived in the 1700s or earlier (see Step _).
- News that an author is writing a family book and that families can indicate how they want to be mentioned in the book, e.g., by initials only, or only ancestors.
- Request for questions from attendees.

Step 18. Lessons Learned on a Genealogy Trip

In May 2021, Kathy Marshall and a cousin met through DNA testing, drove through the State of Georgia searching for their common ancestors. Amy descends from the Marshall slaveholders and Kathy from the Marshall's forced workers who are also blood descendants of those owners. Over a five-day adventure, the cousins spoke about many topics, many of them awkward race-related realities in past and present-day America. They also found common ground and friendly, helpful people wherever they traveled. Through it all, they learned many life lessons together in Georgia, as well as in Alabama, where Kathy traveled alone. Here's a recap of the lessons learned during that trip. They may help you in preparing for your own genealogy trip or Family Harambee event.

The following appeared in Kathy's *Finding Marshalls: A Genealogy Trip with a Black and White Twist* or were experienced in her predecessor book, *The Marshall Legacy in Black and White.*

Tip #1: Examine maps from the places where your family lived

County boundaries often change. Your family may have lived in the same house for generations, but when boundaries change, the official documents may be stored in a different county office nearby.

Tip #2: Keep documents organized

All documents for your family genealogical project should be kept in one place. A good option is a binder labeled by family name with the names of family members on separate tabs within the binder. Arrange all documents chronologically by date. It's also possible to use paper files or digital file folders on a laptop, with each folder labeled with a specific family name. Each digital document should be titled with the family name, the document's year, and a brief description of the file's contents. An example is: Marshall_Joshua_1897_birthcertificate.

Tip #3: Get DNA-tested NOW

Get yourself, your parents, your eldest elders, and first and second cousins DNA-tested NOW. This is especially critical for the descendants of the enslaved, and adoptees, who know little about their family history. DNA, in combination with traditional genealogical research, is a winning combination to find your ancestors. However, it is essential that all participants read and sign an agreement stating whether they want to learn about potentially harmful or upsetting family information. These details might be anything from siblings you didn't know you had to discover you are adopted. You can find one version of the agreement in the Resource section of this workbook.

Tip #4: Closely examine documents related to marriages and inheritances

Check the marriage and probate records of people who married into the family you're researching. Dowries often included enslaved people as gifts, and this information can be found in wills and inventory lists. Other documents may point to periods of indentured servitude for some.

Tip #5: Expect help from our ancestors

When the ancestors want their stories told, they will pave the way for you to get the job done, come sleet, or snow, or officials who withhold necessary paperwork. The ancestors' mandate is for you to do the research, writing, printing, and distributing of their stories—no matter what. Don't let them down.

Tip #6: Plan your itinerary before starting your genealogy trip

Before beginning your genealogy trip, develop an itinerary that includes the places and people you want to visit. Ensure that you determine the hours of operation and availability of venues, as well as make appointments before the visit. Share your plans with family in case they want to join you on the trip or give ideas for more places and people to visit. (See Appendix A).

Tip #7: Develop a list of questions to ask local experts

Develop specific questions for local experts, including asking what they know about the African American community that lived in their area during and after slavery; what research resources they recommend you visit; and whether they are available as guides. Be sure to notify the experts before your trip so they have answers ready and resource materials available during your visit.

Tip #8: Understand the car rental process

Take a deep dive into the car rental process for your destination airport because rental practices differ widely from place to place. On one occasion, the Atlanta airport did not honor Kathy's Express checkout, and that experience delayed her for three hours before she could leave the airport.

Tip #9: Maintain multiple methods of contacting people

Ensure that you have multiple ways to contact your relatives, such as cell and home phone numbers, email, home address, Ancestry account name, Facebook page, and Instagram account, among others. It is debilitating to discover that your method of contact doesn't work and you don't have additional, satisfactory ways of contacting relatives and experts while on your genealogy trip.

Tip #10: Keep a daily journal

Keep a daily diary of your adventures. Describe your feelings and emotions, sights, sounds, and smells, as you find the places where your family lived, or the documents containing your family's information. The journal can be on an electronic device. Typing notes into a computer, laptop, or smartphone every day, instead of writing them longhand, saves you from having to retype them later. Take plenty of photographs and use them to refresh the memory of your experiences. Most of all, enjoy the journey— and record the journey to enjoy it all over again.

Tip #11: Black lives do not always matter

Black lives do not matter in many places in America, even in death, as proven by the large number of unmarked graves in many cemeteries, the continuing police brutality, the rising threats of voter suppression, and on and on. One visceral experience the Kathy experienced during her research learned that the enslaved residents of one town were thrown into a snake-infested bamboo forest in the back of the town's main cemetery. Prepare your emotions!

Tip #12: Fried pickles are tasty!

Try local delicacies to enhance your genealogy experience and memories. An expert from one historical society in Georgia drove Kathy and her cousins all around the county where her family's slave owners had lived in the 1800s. During their lunch break, the group stopped at a BBQ spot that served Georgia's specialty, fried dill pickles. At first skeptical, Kathy was happily surprised at how tasty they were. She enjoyed more local specialties during the trip.

Tip #13: Take plenty of photos and videos

Don't discount any information you glean from a genealogy pilgrimage. Kathy was thankful she had taken photos and video at various cemeteries and at a property where slave owners and her ancestors likely lived. The photos helped her remember details that resulted in believable stories rich with the sights, sounds, and smells from the time and place where her ancestors lived.

Tip #14: Always be aware and alert

Trust your Spidey Sense. Always be aware and alert when traveling to, from, or within unknown places and with new people. Stay present. Remember where you parked your car. Gather and hold on to all of your belongings. Take precautions to avoid becoming a target for possibly unscrupulous locals. Don't be a victim.

Tip #15: Be mindful of your allergies and medical conditions

Stay vigilant of particular animals, insects, flora, fauna, foods that you might be allergic to in your new surroundings. Be sure to pack an inhaler, allergy medicines or other medications and bring them with you on your daily trips and excursions. Consider also packing a small first-aid and sewing kit. You'll be glad you did.

Tip #16: Bring plenty of water and snacks

Ensure you always have enough food and water on your adventures each day to remain hydrated and full of energy. Kathy became delirious and nearly passed out once from dehydration. Don't let that happen to you.

Tip #17: Serendipity can be enlightening

Give in to spontaneity and serendipity, even when it requires a change in your itinerary. Ask locals what their favorite restaurant is, or where they take family who are in town for a visit.Leave some wiggle room in your carefully planned itinerary to take advantage of unplanned experiences and side trips to local attractions.

Tip #18: Honor the Ancestors

Visit cemeteries and other places where your family lived. Take pictures. Take videos of yourself standing in front of sacred spaces to honor your ancestors, as well as well-known monuments and buildings. Bring photos of your family members, place those photos in these sacred ancestral spaces, and record the moment with a photo or video.

Tip #19: Purchase local memorabilia

Purchase something that reminds you of the places you visited, like locally made clothing, jewelry, art or crafts. Visit local artisans, purchase packaged local food delicacies from shops, and allow yourself to fully relish the adventure you're on.

Tip #20: Record professional tours for later

If you are lucky enough to secure an expert guide (contact the local Historical Society or local library for recommendations) be sure to record, photograph, and videotape the tour. A smartphone works well. Back at home, you'll be happy you recorded the tours and can easily transcribe the interviews or edit the clips into a video to share with your family.

Tip #21: Remind travel companions of deadlines

If you are traveling with others, get on the same page about time and appointments. If your travel companion has a completely unique sense of time than you, try to provide multiple reminders of appointments and advance notice of itinerary timetables. Copious amounts of patience and understanding may be necessary to keep tempers cool around agreed-upon deadlines and appointments.

Tip #22: Be empathetic to local customs

Be empathetic to the customs, sights, sounds, sanitation systems, and unusual (to you) food encountered during a genealogy research trip. Another country's or community's way of life is no less valid than our own. For example, a colored (Afro-American) cemetery may be devoid of typical monuments and headstones, because of generations of racism, but that doesn't mean the deceased aren't cherished by their ancestors. Many small towns have a preponderance of people who live in mobile homes, but they shouldn't be regarded as less than those who live in brick and mortar houses.

Tip #23: In-person and online meetings are equally important

A face-to-face or online meeting can go far in fostering loving relationships with family members from different backgrounds. Stories can be shared, differing upbringings brought to light, and the wounds caused by racial divides healed.

Tip #24: Honor the value of Family Harambee events

A concerted effort to find out about your relatives through DNA testing, traditional genealogical research, and Family Harambee get-togethers cements familial relationships. Alex Haley's *Roots: An American Family* shared a view of generational stories that can be shared and discussed during a Family Harambee, helping descendants understand who their ancestors were. Such enlightenment can foster an appreciation of how our ancestors survived the horrific Middle Passage from Africa, the harsh treatment they received as enslaved forced workers in America, and more. Their survival against all odds has allowed their descendants to live (hopefully) better lives now.

Tip #25: Trust your facilitator(s) to resolve conflicts

At a Family Harambee event, in order to air the various sides of your family's stories, install a facilitator whose role will be to encourage a peaceful exchange of ideas. The facilitator would keep conflicting viewpoints from escalating and sinking relationships.

Tip #26: Listen and respect other people's points of view

Always be open to listening to someone else's point of view. Try not to be judgmental if their perspective differs from yours. One of Kathy's White cousins was disappointed by her portrayal of their shared ancestor, a slaveholder, in her book, *The Marshall Legacy in Black and White*. The concerned cousin hailed from a poor White family who had lived among poor Black families. He wrote a lengthy letter describing his family's life of toil and how Blacks and Whites had depended on each other for sustenance and support. Kathy listened attentively to his story, gratified to hear a positive view of race relations she never would have imagined occurring in Georgia.

Tip #27: Check Ahead for Internet Service

Internet service suffers brownouts and worse in some locations. Be sure to plan for alternatives and print out in advance, driving maps and travel routes to the research buildings, cemeteries, and family residences, and other places of interest.

Tip #28: Document your pilgrimage

Write about the day's events in a journal; or create a photo book, paperback, ebook, or audiobook. Use the videos, still photographs, announcements, maps, and other printed materials from each visited location. Create online videos for your family to watch so they feel as though they are visiting the ancestral homeland with you.

Tip #29: Running late? Go anyway!

Even if you're late to a scheduled appointment, go anyway, apologize for your tardiness, say thank you for waiting and maybe bring a small gift of contrition. Enjoy the moment. Better still, confirm the meeting date in advance and don't be late!

Tip #30: Never accept no for an answer

If things aren't going according to plan, come up with creative solutions, like calling or emailing information sources to help achieve your goals. Kathy once avoided a long line outside the courthouse by calling the Deeds office. She was directed to enter a secret entrance that saved her a lot of time.

Tip #31: Be curious

Stop and smell the roses. When unexpected opportunities arise, use them to get more data or to enjoy a novel experience. Driving along State Route 29 in Cotton Valley, Alabama, Kathy pulled off the main road and onto a deserted (and somewhat creepy) side road full of tall, slim trees being grown for a paper mill. A chill rattled through her and she realized that the remote location was possibly unsafe. She drove quickly back to the main road and parked in front of a disbanded post office. As her car stopped, her cell phone rang. Dr. Shari L. Williams was on the line; she had written an article in the *Encyclopedia of Alabama* about Alabama's fourth Lieutenant Governor, Robert Fulwood Ligon. Kathy suspected Lt. Governor Ligon enslaved her great-great-grandmother, Laura Ligon.

Tip #32: Overlay old plat maps onto current highway maps

Plat maps show the division of a piece of land. Get a plat map from the courthouse or library in the community where you are conducting research. The map will detail lots that were purchased by various landowners. Attempt to overlay a present-day map over the plat map and tape it to a window or hold it up to a light so you can see the places your ancestors owned and plan your visit. Consult local experts who can help you. Kathy investigated her great-great-grandparents, Reverend Israel Smith, and his wife, Laura Ligon, who lived in Macon County, Alabama, while enslaved and while free. Several plots in Cotton Valley were owned by former slaveholder, Robert Fulwood Ligon, who may have been Kathy's Ligon family's owner. As she drove on State Route 29 through the area on the map, there were cotton fields as far as her eyes could see. She imagined the days and nights of her Smith and Ligon ancestors.

Tip #33: Talk about your ancestors with everybody

Don't be afraid to talk to strangers about your family and the research you have underway. Say the ancestor's names and the places where they lived. You might just meet someone who is related to you, or who knows someone who might have information about your family. At a Visitor Center on the road back to Atlanta, Kathy told the middle-aged clerk she wanted informational brochures from Talbot and Harris Counties where her Marshall family had lived. He immediately began crying. A woman named Susie Marshall had been his babysitter in Talbot when he was a child. Kathy had taken pictures of every Marshall-surnamed headstone in the cemetery nearest the Marshall slave owner's plantation. One headstone belonged to Susie Marshall—the same woman who took care of the Caucasian clerk. Serendipity inspired goosebumps!

Tip #34: Get help fine-tuning itinerary locations

Gather a group of family members and consult local research centers to fine-tune the list of places to visit and activities to experience on a genealogy trip. It will help you ensure your time is well spent.

Last Words

"One whose seeds have not sprouted does not give up planting."

This African proverb is the guiding light for serious genealogists who don't give up looking for their ancestors even though it is difficult. There's an added level of importance for Afro-American genealogists who feel a driving need to add their ancestral stories to the American historical record because it has long ignored the contributions of African Americans. The workbook provides a practical framework to help families collect, analyze, and discuss their family history and share it with the world.

Family stories may paint a rosier picture than what actually happened. All families must face the possibility of discovering unexpected and potentially controversial details when digging through historical documents in musty courthouse basements and spider-web-by home attics.

DNA is a boon to adoptees and African Americans because genealogy documents are more difficult to find. However, DNA is a double-edged sword, revealing thousands of people who are blood related, whether we already knew about them. Revelations of ethnic and familial background can bring smiles and delight, or shock and loathing. It's essential to learn how to communicate discoveries in a gentle but factual way. This workbook can help families do just that.

Contact Kathy at KathyLynneMarshall.com with questions or to schedule a presentation or workshop.

Purchase Kathy's paperback and e-Books from Amazon. Autographed paperbacks are also available at KathyLynneMarshall.com.

Bibliography

Bennett, Bernice, The Emotional Side of DNA, Midwest African American Genealogy Institute, 2019.

Bettinger, Blaine T., *The Family Tree Guide to DNA Testing and Genetic Genealogy*, Family Tree Books, Cincinnati, OH, 2016.

Bettinger, Blaine T. and Debbie Parker Wayne, *Genetic Genealogy in Practice*, National Genealogical Society Special Topics Series, Arlington, VA, 2016.

DeWolf, Thomas Norman and Sharon Morgan, *Gather at the Table: The Healing Journey of a Daughter of Slavery and a Son of the Slave Trade*, Beacon Press, 2013.

Geddes, Jodie and Tom DeWolf, Coming to the Table: Truth, Justice, Healing, https://comingtothetable.org/

Hansen, Michelle A., *The Complete Family Reunion Planner; Your Start to Finish Workbook for a Fun & Memorable Family Gathering*, Priest Rapids Press.

Marshall, Kathy Lynne, *Finding Marshalls: A Genealogy Trip with a Black and White Twist*, Kanika Marshall Art & Books, 2022.

Marshall, Kathy Lynne, *The Marshall Legacy in Black and White*, Kanika Marshall Art & Books, 2022.

Mayberry, Tiffany, 50+ Conversation Starters for Awkward Family Gatherings, from ApartmentGuide.org at https://www.apartmentguide.com/blog/50-conversation-starters-awkward-family-gatherings/, August 28, 2019.

Mims, Bob, Thousands of genealogy buffs are in Utah for RootsTech — where a new focus on DNA can reveal scandal and surprises, Salt Lake City Tribune, March 2, 2018.

Thompson, Patricia, Dr., 16-page Facilitator's Guide with tips, step-by-step instructions, & resources, silverliningpsychology.com.

Williams, Krystal G., How To Plan Your African-American Family Reunion, Citadel Press, Kensington Publishing Corp, 2000.

Wirthlin, Robin, Healing and the Emotional Side of DNA video, Roots Tech Genealogy Conference, Salt Lake City, Utah, 2020.

Additional Resources available at KathyMarshall.com

About the Author

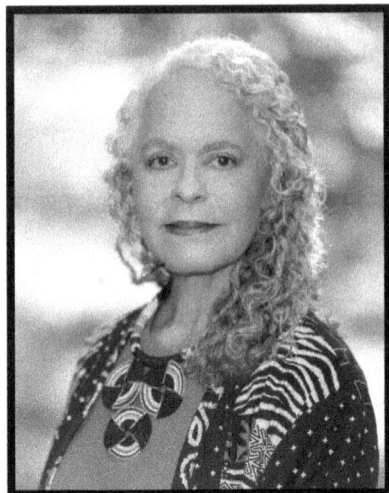

Kathy Lynne Marshall works as a Diversity and Inclusion Specialist on behalf of our ancestors. She's written seven books that enhance the American Historical Record by adding thoroughly researched, factual accounts of the lives of women, enslaved African Americans, and other groups who made America what it is today. All books are available at KathyLynneMarshall.com and online. Five have won book awards, including: *Finding Marshalls: A Genealogy Trip with a Black and White Twist*, *The Marshall Legacy in Black and White*, *The Mystery of Margaret Booker*, *Finding Daisy: From the Deep South to the Promised Land*, and *Finding Otho: The Search for Our Enslaved Williams Ancestors*.

As an instructor, Kathy leads workshops to guide others in writing their family stories. She has been featured in Sacramento Magazine, The Sacramento Bee, The Sacramento Observer, the Sacramento News & Review, Elk Grove Citizen and on Fox40-TV, American Spark-TV and the Research from the National Archives and Beyond podcast. She has delighted audiences at The Sons and Daughters of the United States Middle Passage conference and served as a consultant to West Virginia's Beverly Heritage Center.

An exhibiting artist, Kathy's sculptures have been shown at the Crocker Art Museum, the California State Capitol, the California State Fair Fine Arts Show and in the Maya Angelou Annual Fiber Arts Exhibit in North Charleston, South Carolina.

Want to help your friends and family? Know someone who needs help to leave a written legacy to their children? Give them the gift of one of Kathy Lynne Marshall's biographies or her workbook, available from her KathyLynneMarshall.com website, Amazon and other online book sources.

Please feel free to leave a review for this workbook on Amazon and GoodReads.